FORGING VIRTUE

SHARPENING VALUES, ETHICS, AND SELF AWARENESS

TOM GROGAN
BRENT JURGENSEN

To the arrows in my quiver, Kellan and Elise.
The joy you radiate brings countless smiles to my face. Fly straight,
enjoy the journey, hit your mark.

To Paisley, Royce, and Piper:
What we truly hope to forge with our lives is a legacy. May your
challenges be great, your worthiness be greater, and your heart be
full of joy along the journey. I love you.

CONTENTS

INTRODUCTION

How did we get here?

Necessity is the mother of invention, or so we are told. In the world of education, however, it's not that simple. State and local education departments determine, at minimum, what we will teach and the timeframe we will teach it in. Add in state standards, testing, and other scheduling challenges and things quickly grind to a halt, especially when a fundamental change is on the table. The change we were looking for was to have more impact on the character development of our students, especially our freshman class.

When we were asked to begin teaching a leadership course, our school labeled it "Leadership and Ethics". Little did we know where that title itself would lead. Each year it looked and felt different, for us *and* the students. The first year was highly technical work (try teaching deontological thought and reasoning to 15-year-olds), but the students jumped completely in, and we were reminded of the importance of personalizing the learning process, especially when we were constantly asking the students to self-evaluate. The next year, we shifted more toward philosophy and acts of service. It improved our ability as teachers to relate to the students, but the rigor that we were also accustomed to was not there.

What really started to change the tide, however, was when we invited other community and school leaders into our classroom. Fellow teachers, business and entrepreneurial pioneers, and even the Speaker of the House of our state legislature spoke to our students. We had dedicated hours and hours to developing content, and yet these leaders brought an entirely new perspective to what we were teaching and how we could instantly improve our practices. It was humbling, encouraging, and frustrating all at the same time. So we channeled that energy into refining the course again. We turned to Maslow, Plato, Socrates, Manson (Mark, that is), Brene Brown, David Brooks, Simon Sinek, and a host of other writers and thought leaders. Our organization and content definitely improved, but we felt like we were still missing something.

Enter Joseph Campbell. Campbell's decades of work with mythology, symbology, and most importantly, *The Hero's Journey*, was the key we needed to unlock the door. Students all know the journey; they see it in every movie and book. The examples of how to incorporate pieces of philosophy and character education into our class served as the last aspect of the picture that we desperately needed. Everything was aligned and finally moving in the same direction. More than 40 students each semester were receiving what we felt was the very best we had to offer.

Then the class was dropped from the schedule.

Years of effort didn't feel necessarily wasted, but certainly misplaced. How were we going to use the information, activities, and lessons that we had developed in our regular classrooms? Fortunately, another opportunity presented itself, and we were tasked with providing a character education curriculum for our homeroom classes. It was a bit of a different focus from what we had previously done, but something we certainly felt we could handle. Our first thought was to find a book or program that we could simply apply to our school. By including our school's values and goals with whatever resource we found, we were positive we could meet and exceed expectations.

But the problem quickly became clear. For all of the self-help, philosophy, social-emotional learning, and character development books out there, we could not find a single one that facilitated *genuine* discussions with high school students. Even worse, the topics and "ethical dilemmas" that we continued to find were either focused on younger students or were so deep and emotional that it would be incredibly difficult to condense a lesson of that magnitude into a 25-minute period once a week. So that's how we got here — necessity actually *is* the mother of invention.

Now, a year and a half later, we have written the book we needed but couldn't find. We took ideas from the best modern thinkers around, combined it with aspects from classic philosophers and pieces of the "hero's journey", and organized them in a way that any adult could use, teacher or parent, coach or mentor. Our goal was to provide opportunities to have the authentic conversations with kids that they so desperately need. Positive, meaningful human interaction has decreased significantly in the last decade. We see it every day in our classrooms. It is our most fervent hope that our book can open the door to those meaningful discussions while also providing a path for students to learn who they are — or, more importantly, who they can become.

Modern society values the ability of people to transition quickly into the working world. Education is set up to have students be college or career ready. But to meet that end, students have not been taught how to function in an equally modern society. Social media addictions have replaced the days of latch-key kids and neighborhood schools. Kids are more isolated than they ever have been before, even though they are more "connected". We believe that the values, skills, and questions ahead will guide adults and students to an actual connection, one that is tethered in trust, compassion, humility, and gratitude. We have written this book to fill our professional need, but as you read it, we hope that it will become what we all should strive to be: a gift.

Best of luck on your journey! We are proud and honored to be with you the entire way. The path to self-awareness begins with integrity, a virtue that serves as the cornerstone for all others. It ends, as all journeys do, with gratitude and a sense of accomplishment, but more importantly, responsibility to do more. Consider this book our effort to fulfill that responsibility, knowing full well that it is actually the first step toward another adventure.

HOW TO USE THIS BOOK

Human beings are inherently collaborative. Working together has been an essential part of our species from day one. For thousands of years we have refined, reshaped, and revised our abilities to work together in the most efficient way possible. For generations, people have questioned the complexity of our relationships, and each generation, they have found answers. And yet, those answers never quite satisfied the next generation. In our present age, we do not differ from our ancestors. During the height of each powerful ancient civilization, people would sit and ponder deep questions about who we are and how to live a more fulfilling life. Today, we refer to these people as philosophers. In ancient times, philosophers would sit and discuss for hours, days, months, and sometimes a lifetime about questions leading to deeper purpose and the meaning to life. They focused many of their discussions on characteristics that influenced behavior. Today, we refer to these characteristics as values.

There are SO MANY values identified today. Our goal in this book is not to discuss them all. Instead, we chose a list of values that we feel are essential to building a sound foundation for the development of self-awareness, social awareness, relationship building, and strong decision making.

There are eight parts to this book. We wrote each part to build on the previous, like building scaffolding for a structure. Because of this, bouncing around from one part to another will be less effective than working through the book from beginning to end.

Within each part, there are three chapters. The chapters highlight why the specific value is important and what the optimal uses of that value are in our day-to-day lives. Because our values are so complex and personal, however, we believe there are frequently a number of values at work continuously. The chapters themselves are filled with a variety of values and skills. We believe that when we are at our best, our values are all working together. Our individual values are important to develop, but the stacking of multiple values leads to maximizing our potential.

After teaching content similar to this book for years, it is our opinion that the best learning happens through discussion. For many kids, help will be needed to navigate through this material. Most times, there will be a lot of SILENCE. Patience will be the key here. Taking time to process our thoughts about new and complicated material is perfectly normal and encouraged.

Furthermore, questions have been raised about "finding the answers" to some of the most difficult questions throughout the book. Every journey is unique in its own way. It is our hope that this book will be a resource to *help* you forge your own path, not forge the path for you. We believe it would be impractical and complicated to try to provide solutions to persons and situations that we don't know or understand.

Each chapter has three questions and usually one activity to work through. Discussing the questions and activities will be essential to personal development! The primary purpose of this book is to provide a jumping-off point to promote genuine conversations.

We conclude each chapter with sections about traps and champions. The words "In the fire" and "Forged" symbolize the refinement to become a virtuous person. We believe personal growth is difficult and extensive. "In the fire" refers to *some* of our intentional and unintentional choices that deter us from fully embodying the value. The "Forged" sections outline *some* ways each value is being lived out to its full potential. Again, the intention of these sections is to help start conversations.

You will also read sections called "Sharpen Your Edge," as seen below. These sections are meant for readers to stop and reflect about what they just read or to participate in an activity for further development. These reflections will usually take a minute or two, but in some cases, they can take hours, days, or possibly longer to complete. When you get to these activities, allow some time to work through them. If more time is needed, it is perfectly fine to take a break and come back to it later.

Sharpen Your Edge

---

1. WHAT DO YOU NEED TO DO DAILY?

2. WHAT CHALLENGES WILL YOU FACE?

3. WHO CAN HELP SUPPORT YOU?

While in the fire, using this book looks like....

Fear

You're afraid to teach the contents of this book because you don't fully understand. This is normal. It took us years before we, as adults, could talk deeply about some of this stuff. Don't take our word for it. One of Socrates' most famous quotes was "I know, that I don't know."

Time restraints

Time can become an issue in teaching, discussing, etc. It is our observation that conversations about this type of content are happening less and less. Something is better than nothing. Use whatever time you have - it will make a difference.

Lack of interest

Sometimes kids get nervous and don't participate in the discussions. Believe it or not, they are interested, especially in understanding themselves. Forcing kids to share can be a dangerous game. If listening is what they need, let them listen. If no one is speaking, reword your questions or approach the topic from a different angle. Occasionally, it's best to have that silence to allow the students and yourself the space to work through more ideas. Providing an opportunity to share their thoughts and feelings through other mediums can be very beneficial. Some of the most reserved kids have produced the most powerful writings, artwork, and service projects.

Jump around guy

Try to work through this book in order. This book was written to gradually get deeper. However, you're in charge! Use it as you see fit!

When using this book, it will Forge...

An atmosphere of trust

Creating a sense of trust is paramount. It is hard for anyone to share personal feelings when they can't trust people around them. Every opinion, story, or remark that is shared should be heard and valued. Oftentimes, the remarks that seem the most bonkers will lead to the best discussions.

Other resources

We are the first to admit that this book does not have all the answers. This is certainly not a one-size-fits-all book. Find the best resources to help you. This is just a guide. Find and use what you think will work best for your situation.

Fun

Have fun! Those around you will feed off your energy. If you're not into it, they won't be either. Relax, smile, and take pride in knowing that you are helping to shape them into better people.

The sharing of stories

Be willing to share your story. No one knows your story better than you. Share it! The personal insight and narrative you can bring to a moment of learning is pure gold. It is the hinge by which all relationships, especially mentoring relationships, are fixed.

PART I

INTEGRITY

An interesting place to begin, integrity has plenty of definitions, especially the "what you do when no one is watching" version. In fact, when we would ask students to answer the question "what is integrity", that was the most common answer we received. It is easily, in our opinion, the worst definition out there. It takes zero courage to do the right thing when you're alone. This is what makes understanding integrity so challenging. It can easily be confused or conflicting with ideas of morality (doing the right thing instead of wrong) and integrity (becoming the living embodiment OF your morals, values, and virtues). It takes immense amounts of courage to do the right thing, especially when it's not the popular thing, when everyone is watching. It is the ultimate "what are you made of" moment. This section addresses the parts of integrity— wholeness, honor, and virtues— that will give us all the will to act with integrity, regardless of the situation.

. . .

Wholeness presents the individual as three parts; the body, the mind, and the soul. Having each component of wholeness aligned and reflecting our values is an excellent start to knowing how we are going to act from day one. While certainly not simple or easy, kids will quickly become aware of what makes them tick in each way.

Honor gives us "the code". That "code" is the blueprint that gives us a better understanding of right and wrong, when we know who we are, and where we came from. Identifying important people in our lives and why they are important gives us insight into how to act when they aren't around.

Virtues are simply values in action. Wholeness and honor lead the way to discovering our individual values, but acting upon those values is what begins our work toward becoming more self-aware.

So, what *are* you made of?

1

WHOLENESS

"A true desire is not to have, but to be. We are whole creatures in potential, and the true purpose of desire is to unfold that wholeness, to become what we can."

— ERIC BUTTERWORTH

WHAT DOES IT MEAN TO BE CONNECTED?

Every epic tale begins with one step. That one step sets the direction down a specific path that will lead to your becoming a more polished version of yourself. But when we take that first step, we must be connected to our physical world in that moment to know we are there to take a step toward our future, better self.

We are all a different story. Our stories shape and define us. Some tales recount joy, happiness, celebrations and achievement. Others crush our emotions. Stories of abuse, neglect, absence, and loneliness leave us trying to piece any part of it back together. People find themselves somewhere in between, trying to balance the positive with the negative, while also trying to figure out who they are. Though your story does matter in terms of how you arrived at this moment, you write your own story as soon as you know where you are and where you want to be.

Your life comprises two primary entities; you and those who are within your circle. Think of it this way; when building skyscrapers, teams of men had to walk the high beams and scaffolding before the base and internal structure of the building could begin. The same is true for us. By collecting the right builders and designers around us in the best "location," we can build the framework we will need for the work that lies ahead.

Our people - our friends, collaborators, and critics - ensure that we are connected in all we do. They understand where we currently are and listen when we tell them where we want to be. By grounding us in the present, they make sure we have what we need to grow. Being physically present means we are aware of those people, our surroundings, and how they all influence the way we think, speak, and act. Before we can think about other aspects of wholeness, we must be diligent about being connected and physically present as much as possible.

An active, present mind is a significant challenge. We see plenty of outer distractions, not to mention all the internal conversations we navigate. Understanding how we perceive things can go a long way in syncing our thoughts with our physical presence and awareness.

Visualization of goals and goal-setting are two practices to clear our minds for the present and the future. Life events and our reactions to them create our understanding of the world. Our perception becomes pre-programmed by a lifetime of inputs. How those influences mold our understanding of our own thoughts and emotions makes all the difference when we are trying to align our mind, body and spirit.

Mark Manson describes this by using a car analogy. Paraphrasing his theory, we acknowledge a few things that we feel are true, but might not want to admit. First, we are "driven" by our emotions. No matter how much we try to convince ourselves that we are logical and don't give in to emotion, it just isn't true. Manson argues that our logic side of the brain tries to convince the emotional driver of our brain to act, not the other way around. So until we understand that, we must use logic to keep our emotions somewhat in check, or "driving in the right direction", we will struggle with the power and range of our emotions. The sooner we accept this as a truth for ourselves, the sooner we understand our emotions and thoughts differently.[1]

As we grow mentally, we want to gain awareness of our emotions, the source of those emotions, the way we attach meaning to those emotions, and finally, how far we will let them "drive" us before logic must step in to keep us on the road.

When we are doing our best daily, both in body and in mind, we contribute to the overall integrity or wholeness of those around us and ourselves. This has nothing to do with how smart you are, what your last name is, or what you did yesterday. It has everything to do with showing up today, ready to grow, and preparing as much as you can to look for opportunities to evolve with every passing moment. But the last piece isn't physical or emotional. It is deeply spiritual.

The Statue of Liberty in New York has stood as a literal beacon of freedom since opening in 1886. The over 300ft structure was the tallest building in New York for a time. A gift from France commemorating the centennial of the Declaration of Independence, Lady Liberty is one of the first structures vessels see on the way into the Port of New York. Her copper exterior quickly turned the green that we now see today. But it is a poem from 1883 that gave the statue "life".

"The New Colossus" by Emma Lazarus gave the statue the one piece of the puzzle that was missing; a soul. Calling her the "Mother of Exiles," Lazarus proclaimed the statue to be the symbol of freedom and opportunity for all, but especially those who had struggled the most. It enshrines the words with the statue's purpose, essentially giving her life.

The "spirit" work that we need to do connects the physical and emotional traits that we have, while also connecting us to everyone else in our lives. It is the essence of who we all are. The soul, or spirit, we all have encourages us to explore our passions and interests. It pushes us to find new and meaningful relationships, even if those relationships don't turn out so well.

Our internal compass also leads us toward finding our values and virtues because we can validate them with those around us. We find our purpose, our passions, and our future by combining our mind, body, and spirit.

Sharpen Your Edge

---

1. WHERE DO YOU FEEL MOST "PRESENT" OR COMFORTABLE? CAN YOU CREATE THAT ENVIRONMENT WHEREVER YOU GO? HOW?

2. WHAT DO YOU DO WHEN YOUR MIND IS RACING AND WON'T QUIET DOWN? HOW ARE YOU ABLE TO RECOGNIZE YOUR EMOTIONS? IN WHAT WAYS DO THEY CONTROL YOU, AND VICE VERSA?

3. WHAT ARE YOU MOST CONNECTED TO THAT ALSO CONNECTS YOU TO OTHER PEOPLE (IE. MUSIC, THEATER, ART, SPORTS, ETC?) HOW DO YOU FEEL WHEN YOU EXPERIENCE SOMETHING WITH A GROUP OF OTHER PEOPLE?

WHILE IN THE FIRE, WHOLENESS LOOKS LIKE....

CONCRETE SHOES

"It's just easier to stay where we are." New things mean new expectations, and that makes us uncomfortable. When we change our connections or location (where we live, work, go to school, etc.), we immediately become defensive, suspicious, and invulnerable, all of which are the opposite of growth. So instead, we stay in our comfort zone, our bubble, and keep the world at bay. Same view, same conversations, same meals.

ROAD RAGE

We let our emotions "take the wheel," leading us everywhere except where we need to go. Emotions are with us for everything. Instead of acknowledging that we have feelings, sometimes we just push them down until they force their way to the surface. Once that happens, they control everything we say and do, and frequently, that's not a good scenario.

EMPTY VESSELS

Silence is scary to many, many people. So instead of burrowing into that quiet place and doing some soul searching, we increase the volume from the outside world. By doing this, we miss opportunities to center ourselves and connect on a deeper level. This also leaves us feeling empty and alone.

WHEN WHOLENESS IS FORGED, IT WILL...

"LACE 'EM UP!"

Seek fresh possibilities. Find the best place for you physically to be and you can grow. Take that first step! Force yourself to see things from a new perspective or position. Read books that take you to a far away place and put you in the shoes of someone you have never met.

BREAK THE CODE

Try to understand how your perceptions and influences, including your own thoughts and emotions, affect everything around you. Investigate your ideas and feelings for where they are coming from, and you will have a clearer understanding of your mind and thought process. Then you can make it work for you.

FILL THE BUCKET

Find people and activities that nourish your "soul"- your passions, interests, and values. Work on deepening your relationship with yourself first to work closer to the idea of becoming whole. Find solace in the silence by meditating, taking a yoga class at the gym, or getting back into one of your favorite hobbies. Each activity will give you a clearer view into who you are and what you want to become.

2

HONOR

"No person was ever honored for what he received. Honor has been the reward for what he gave."

— CALVIN COOLIDGE

"IN WORD AND IN DEED"...

When we think of the concept of honor in America, we usually associate it with the members of our military. In fact, the Medal of Honor is the highest honor awarded in the United States Armed Forces. It is reserved for those soldiers who demonstrated courage beyond comparison, and always is a result of a selfless act to benefit others. In Japan, the Samurai warrior was the defender of the shogunate and prefecture. They followed a strict honor code to maintain the integrity of their order. In both instances, death was preferable to acting in a dishonorable manner. The exemplar of honor in western society can be found in the open lands of Europe.

We find the equivalent to the way of the Samurai in the Code of Chivalry. Documented in 1100 A.D., the Knight's Code of Chivalry described what it meant to be a knight. The code included protecting the weak, aide widows and orphans, fight for the welfare of all, guard the honor of fellow knights, keep the faith, honor women, and never refuse a challenge from an equal. To this day, knights are symbols of virtue and courage. They have the physical strength to defend themselves from any foe, yet they find their truest purpose in defending others. Knights don't act for personal gain, but for the benefit of their "lord" and their community. While we don't see the actual "knight in shining armor" today, we certainly have people, both in our lives and in the world as a whole, who represent the honorable actions associated with chivalry and knighthood.

WHO IS SOMEONE YOU WOULD NEVER WANT TO DISAPPOINT?

Exercise unwavering commitment to the people and ideals you choose to live by. There are many ways and times to compromise; loyalty to those who have helped you is not among them.

- Honor your parents.
- Honor your grandparents.
- Honor your mentors.
- Honor your family.

When we have asked this question to students, the most common answer is usually a parent or grandparent. It makes total sense! We immediately recognize the people it would hurt the most if we did something really dumb or even worse, immoral and wrong. What we usually fail to realize is that guilt doesn't come from nowhere; rather it comes from an unconscious realization of how much they have actually invested <u>in</u> us. Think about that and enjoy the wave of guilt and shame that comes with it!

Just kidding.

Actually, not kidding. It's a real thing. So how can we use this realization to improve our actions the next time we are forced into that uncomfortable ethical dilemma?

Understand that you have a piece of every one of these groups inside of your character. Honor them with your thoughts, words, and actions. Dishonoring them and your community is arguably the worst thing you can do. We dishonor these people by lying, cheating, and behaving in unethical ways. Conduct yourself to make others proud of you. Act in a way that people will KNOW that you are a person of honor!

HOW DO WE KNOW HOW TO ACT WITH HONOR?

Look to the people who have helped you the most or where you spend the most time.

We all have a different family story, but we all go to the same school, same job, etc., every single day. We should have consistent discussions and opportunities to determine what our **VALUES** are. Are you being respectful and courteous? Are you acting with integrity, being honest, even honorable?

Every institution, whether it's your family, your school, your church, or your team, has pillars that guide their behavior.

Are you doing and saying things that you and your class-mates/teachers will be proud of? How do you know?

Are you striving to be better today than you were yesterday? How do you measure your growth?

Are you doing these things through honest effort and not taking shortcuts? How do you know the difference between the two?

If you can answer both "yes" and how you can "prove" your answer, you are honoring what we consider important values in our society. If not, start today. Better habits begin on Day One, not one day.

WHY IS HONOR AN IMPORTANT PART OF CHARACTER?

Honor lets everyone around you know you are dependable and that you are an example of how "good" we can be.

Knights were the best. At everything— smart, kind, strong, patient, faithful, humble, and many other things. A knight chose that life, and in doing so became a champion of those ideas. They never fought others for personal glory; rather they fought to defend the people and values of their kingdom or community. Think of the movies and stories you know that have a knight as a villain. The bad guys only use their strength and wisdom for personal gain. They cheat others out of their money, happiness, and maybe even their life. And they always have black armor, showing that they are evil and impure (Hello, Darth Vader!) They once had the virtues of a knight but became selfish and power hungry. "A Jedi you no longer are" (insert Yoda voice here).

Be the knight of your realm. Honor those who have come before you.[1]

Honor the privilege of being part of this incredible journey, in word and in deed!

WHILE IN THE FIRE, HONOR LOOKS LIKE....

DISHONOR

Guilt trip, engage! Hearing "I'm not mad, I'm just very disappointed" is a brutal gut punch to anyone, but especially when it comes from a person we respect and cherish. Unfortunately, as we learn about ourselves and how we are going to make decisions, we are going to mess up. On the most severe level, our actions actually dishonor those who have come before us and invested in us. It's a mistake we all make, but also one we cannot afford to repeat.

DISCONNECTION

We aren't "grounded" in any person, belief, or idea. As human beings, we struggle the most when we don't feel like we belong—to anyone or anything. The internet and your phone don't count either. When we do things we aren't proud of, we usually push people away, making the cause of those actions an even bigger problem.

THE DARK SIDE

Not like Darth Vader dark, but maybe showing some early signs? No, not really, but we are certainly shying away from the "light" when we don't act in a way that we know is right or good. We discredit the impact we can have, so we don't see or understand the effect we have on others.

WHEN HONOR IS FORGED, IT WILL...

STRENGTHEN LOYALTY

We fight the good fight and we know how! Knowing that we are a reflection of those who have raised or mentored us is an important first step. By understanding this, we consider our actions before we take them, ensuring that we would never act to embarrass the people, and even ideas, that we value the most.

ENCOURAGE VULNERABILITY

We are confident in "who we are and who we belong to." That's a fancy way of saying "we get it. Don't do things that will embarrass ourselves, our families, etc." Even more so, we are willing to express the values that our families and institutions have provided. We demonstrate our gratitude to family and friends by being the best example of the values and virtues we have been taught.

RAISE THE BANNER

We embody the spirit and values of our communities. While we continue to grow and learn, our most important responsibility is toward the betterment of others. We are now a symbol of what we represent and we are proud of who we are and what we are becoming.

3

VIRTUES

"All that I see is what I am not"

— Anonymous

THERE ARE MANY, MANY PEOPLE WHO IDENTIFY WITH THAT QUOTE; some certainly more than others, but it is absolutely something we all have thought. We are usually our greatest critics, and many times that criticism is much too severe, and possibly inaccurate. Why do we have such a strong tendency to do that?

WHAT ARE FLAWS, ANYWAY?

Where to begin with this question...

Let's start here: No one is perfect. Accepting that truth lets us begin looking at ourselves in a way that seeks chances to grow rather than limit what we are.

Think of a diamond. A diamond is one of the most precious stones on the planet. However, even the perfect stone has to be cut, cleaned, and shaped to increase its overall worth and appeal. The reshaping of the diamond brings out its greatest qualities while working to eliminate the chips or nicks that come with the pressure and reshaping that happens while it is formed. You and I are no different.

We all have our scars, bad habits, and challenges that we deal with as kids and adults. Finding these flaws is where many of us stop looking. We see the perceived imperfection and see it as something that will always be in the way. Even worse, that frequently turns into us pointing out the flaws in others in hopes of not having our scars and scrapes exposed. In truth, it's those flaws that will point us in the right direction for any part of our lives that we would like to improve.

It's also important to note that we don't want you to read this and think "Well I already know I'm not perfect and I don't want to hear it from someone else." Or, "I'm awesome, I don't need to worry about it." Listen, the point is, how are you going to make yourself better? There is a process and the process is going to be challenging.

. . .

HOW DO WE UNDERSTAND WHAT FLAWS WE HAVE?

Good news. This is actually much easier than it was to accept the number of flaws we have. And it focuses on the best, most positive parts of your life!

Priorities are what we consider the most important part of our day. Depending on what those priorities are, we will get up at a certain time, dress a certain way, eat certain foods, interact with specific people, etc. Priorities are essentially a filtering system that we develop in order to decide and think about what we are doing or not doing. Without this process we would just spin in circles, chasing our tail hoping to get somewhere but not really moving at all. This might feel like a familiar pattern to some or many young people. Many adults you see continue to spin this way in one aspect of their lives or another. So it only makes sense for us to move forward by first figuring out what our priorities actually are.

Grab a paper and pencil and start writing what you would consider the top four priorities in your life as you sit here today. We make this process much more simple by writing in complete sentences. You might think to yourself, why are you asking me to write this? Well, formulating a complete thought, and writing it down is an old trick to help you remember information later. Also, writing forces you to think longer and help *prioritize* what's really important. So, what are your top priorities?

HERE ARE SOME SIMPLE EXAMPLES:

"Being a good daughter to my parents."

"Being a good sister to my siblings."

. . .

ALRIGHT. NOW THAT YOU HAVE THOSE WRITTEN, TAKE SOME TIME to think about *why* you actually wrote those specific words to describe your priorities. Write that down as well. *Why* are these my priorities? Here is an example with the why component:

"Being a good daughter to my parents and sister to my siblings is important to me because I love them and I want to earn their respect and provide an example to my brother and sister".

What words stand out in the sentence above that would give me a clear understanding of why that is a priority to me? Underline them.

"Being a <u>good daughter</u> to my parents and <u>sister</u> to my siblings is important to me because I <u>love</u> them and I want to earn their <u>respect</u> and provide an <u>example</u> to my brother and sister".

In looking at what I underlined, I can now see that my priorities reflect a series of specific traits that I feel are the most important, otherwise known as my <u>values</u>. <u>Daughter</u> and <u>sibling</u> reflect the value of **accountability** to others. <u>Love</u> reflects how I feel that I can **communicate** my values to my family. <u>Respect</u> is reflected in earning the **esteem** of my family. <u>Example</u> reflects what we call **legacy**, or what others will remember about me well after I'm gone. This portion of the chapter is going to take some time, but we promise it will give you precious insight into yourself.

WHAT DO PRIORITIES AND VALUES HAVE TO DO WITH VIRTUES?

Tackling the "value" question marks an important milestone for you in your evolution into who you want to become. Because those values are also verbs, they imply an action being taken. In that moment of movement, they become virtues.

We won't go overboard with the history of virtues here, but

an excellent place to gain an understanding of virtues comes from Plato and Socrates. While Plato discussed the importance of virtues in a community or city, he felt it was also important that each individual person work on these virtues to create a better version of themselves.

For example, in his book *The Republic*, Plato asserts that there are three common virtues between states and their citizens; wisdom, courage, and moderation.

WISDOM IS KNOWLEDGE THAT IS PASSED ON OR GAINED THROUGH actively listening to others.

COURAGE IS THE COMBINATION OF A BELIEF (OR FOR OUR discussion, a value) and steadfastness in character.

MODERATION (KNOWING WHEN ENOUGH IS ENOUGH) IS A VIRTUE that promotes order and harmony.

BY PRACTICING THESE THREE VIRTUES, INDIVIDUALS AND communities alike found common ground and the ability to grow through and with each other. As humans, we grow the most when we involve other people (relationships) and work through and with them to reach new heights. These three virtues create an understanding of justice. As we continue to grow and apply virtues to our daily lives, we have a clearer understanding of those things that we consider unjust and how we strive to fix them.

The beauty of these virtues lies in their simplicity and their effectiveness when used in all aspects of life. Exploring the world to gain more knowledge, having conviction and belief in yourself and what you believe to be good, and learning to balance your life are all key to your development and ultimately what many people would consider happiness.

SOUNDS SIMPLE, RIGHT? SO WHY AREN'T MORE PEOPLE DOING this?

IT ALL GOES BACK TO THE QUOTATION AT THE BEGINNING OF THE chapter. People fixate on what they are not, rather than what they can become. Changing our perception of flaws can make a tremendous difference in our chances to learn about ourselves.

Simply put, flaws are those aspects of our life that are limiting our effectiveness and potential growth. You could be a talented writer, but you don't take the time to write, or you continually talk yourself out of it. You believe in helping others, but won't take that first step to volunteer unless someone goes with you. These are the easy ones. Some of you have to work through recent traumas in order to move forward. In other cases, it might mean forgiving someone who has hurt you, or apologizing for something you aren't exactly proud of mentioning again.

Ultimately, we must choose to be working closer to those aspects of our life that are limiting our greatness. Call them flaws, personality traits, terrible luck, whatever it may be, we have to know what our values and virtues are in order to identify our flaws accurately. We can then begin the process of remaking those aspects of our lives.

As the Persian poet Rumi said, "The wound is the place where the Light enters you." To become a better person, we need to seek out these "wounds" first, letting them guide the way to our light.

Sharpen Your Edge

I. WHAT FLAWS ARE THE MOST COMMON AMONGST YOU AND YOUR FRIENDS? DO YOU LIMIT THE EFFECTS OF THOSE FLAWS, OR DO YOU PICK UP FLAWS FROM THEM?

2. FLAWS ARE NOT FAILURES! THEY ARE PIECES THAT CAN BE POLISHED INTO A STRENGTH. MAKE SURE THAT THEY ARE YOUR FLAWS, THOUGH. WE HAVE TO OWN THEM BEFORE WE CAN WORK ON THEM.

3. BEING VULNERABLE ABOUT OUR SHORTCOMINGS CAN BE A TOUGH THING FOR ANYONE TO DO, ESPECIALLY IF WE ARE IN A GROUP. ANY ACTIVITY LIKE THIS SHOULD BE CONDUCTED WITH THE OPPORTUNITY TO COMPLETE IT WITHOUT BEING READ IN FRONT OF THE GROUP, AND MAYBE EVEN READ BY THE LEADER. THIS BUILDS TRUST AND DEMONSTRATES RESPECT FOR THE WORK THE KIDS ARE DOING.

WHILE IN THE FIRE, VIRTUE LOOKS LIKE....

BAND AIDES AND MAKE-UP

Instead of seeing our flaws as a chance to grow, we are ashamed of them and try to cover them up. We don't embrace being vulnerable with ourselves, instead focusing on the flaws of others.

IT'S UNTETHERED

We really lack the ability to see the impact we have on others. We also don't have the courage to be honest with ourselves about the things we hold most dear or are most afraid of. We aren't connected, or tethered, to people or ideas that keep us grounded and "in the moment".

BEING STUCK IN NEUTRAL

Values become virtues by acting on them. If we don't act on our values, we will never understand what priorities we have and how we can set goals to improve upon them.

WHEN VIRTUE IS FORGED, IT WILL...

OWN FLAWS

Flaws are a part of who we, and everyone else, are. We see them as part of the process that got us to this point. Rather than being ashamed of them, we use our flaws to seek out the truth of who we can become.

PRIORITIZE PEOPLE

We seek ways to make sure that the people in our lives know how important they are to us. The effort to become more engaged with people in a positive way points us in the right direction to find our values. That guidance makes it easier for us to work toward our goals and put those values into actions.

CONNECT THE DOTS

The champion of virtues has begun using the values they identified in themselves. They see how they can improve themselves and their relationships with others, and they actively seek opportunities to prove it.

PART II

HUMILITY

Humility is the foundation for all learning. It is woven into the very fabric of success in all parts of life. Humility is the willingness to accept wisdom, knowledge, and guidance...even when you think you know a lot.

In my experience, there is far too much confusion with young people about this critical value. Humility is NOT humiliation. We often equate humiliation with shame, an emotion no person in their right mind would want to embrace. On the contrary, humility embraces potential failures because they can inevitably lead to growth. Humility will always require a sacrifice of ego. Oftentimes, that sacrifice can feel humiliating, uncomfortable, or even a bit foolish. The antidote to the fear of being wrong or looking "bad" is our support system. Active collaboration is the backbone of achievement which requires humility—admitting that you can't do everything alone.

. . .

Self-Esteem and Failure might sound negative at first. A closer look reveals that failure is part of any worthwhile process, and our self-esteem is dramatically improved when we understand how our failures can teach us.

Sacrifice is an essential part of success of any kind. The willingness to accept sacrifice, particularly knowing what to sacrifice, and when, can be helpful in our pursuit of greatness.

Achievement is not just a result of our own doing. Rather, a humble look at who has helped us achieve our goals paints a clearer picture of our lives and our constant need for each other. It takes individual effort, as well as the support of others, to achieve.

4

SELF-ESTEEM AND FAILURE

"Success is not built on success. It's built on failure. It's built on frustration. Sometimes it's built on catastrophe."

— SUMNER REDSTONE

WE LIVE IN A WORLD WHERE WE ARE JUDGED MORE BY OUR digital image than by what we present in actual life. How many Instagram posts or Snapchat streaks have ended because the perfect picture wasn't available? We don't value *actual* accomplishments of *actual* people. Rather, we talk about *Call of Duty* killstreaks, followers, and the latest gossip about so-and-so's posts.

None of it is real. So how do we accomplish things in real life when our experiences have never taught us how to do just that? First, we have to see why the self-esteem experiment of the last thirty years has not had its intended consequences. Second, we need to have a healthy understanding of what failure is and its purpose in our lives. Finally, we have to connect the dots between actual failures and how they build our image and feelings of self-worth (also known as self-esteem).

HOW HAS OVER-PRAISE DAMAGED SELF-ESTEEM AND PRIDE?

The self-esteem movement of the late 1980s and early 1990s tried to remove the heartbreak of failure from school, activities, and life in general.

All the likes, hearts, thumbs-up, and retweets you've gotten come from a real person, but those digital affirmations don't actually exist.

We all know when we haven't done our best, or even close to our best. Our friends and family will come up to us and say "Good job!", we say "Thank you", then walk off telling ourselves, "Yeah, right! I was terrible!" Being praised for underachieving or not achieving at all has become the way we do things. Getting credit for just doing a job has replaced doing your best.

We have confused praise and self-esteem. We became so

afraid of telling people the truth or even talking about the idea of failure that we shifted to lying about what really happened!

Pride directly results from accomplishing something. Accomplishment comes via trying something over and over again, even after failing at that same task. We won't have the patience or incentive to try again and again if we don't accept that failure is part of the process, not the end of it.

HOW DOES THE FEAR OF FAILURE IMPEDE OUR WILLINGNESS TO TRY?

It's almost impossible for us to go through life without experiencing failure.

Failure is entirely defined by how we look at it.

Unfortunately, failure is often seen in a negative light. There is a tremendous amount of anxiety associated with failure. Feelings of pain, remorse, regret, and guilt are often emotions we run from. However, when you stop and think about the long-term effects of failure, it should be seen as life's great teacher.

"You learn a line from a win, and a book from defeat"
-Paul Brown

Failure should never be our sole motivation to not try. But let's get one thing clear: there is a distinct difference between destructive failure and constructive failure. Destructive failure involves decisions that might destroy you as a person physically, emotionally, and/or spiritually. Constructive failures are shortfalls toward your purpose and vision. The "healthy" failures are those that provide construction toward your purpose and vision.

In your pursuits toward your goals and dreams, fear of failure is inevitable and at times can be paralyzing to your decision-making. However, reflecting with a few stop-and-think questions can help navigate the fear.

Sharpen Your Edge

STOP-AND-THINK QUESTIONS

1. HAVE YOU ANALYZED EVERY POTENTIAL OUTCOME?

2. ARE YOU ONLY LOOKING AT THIS WITH A NEGATIVE LENS?

3. WHAT IS THE WORST-CASE SCENARIO?

SOMETIMES, THE RESULT MAY BE DISASTROUS. IN MOST CASES, HOWEVER, THE WORST CASE MAY NOT BE THAT BAD. DO YOU HAVE A CONTINGENCY PLAN?

HOW DO FAILURES ACTUALLY LEAD TO SELF-ESTEEM?

Failure is the only road to self-esteem. You cannot get self-esteem from others...it's not called others-esteem.

Self-esteem is a person's perception of their physical self-image, their accomplishments and capabilities, and their values. In life, we are constantly making choices to pursue new skills to develop our self-esteem and self-worth. In the back of our minds that little voice is chirping, reminding us of the potential failures or shortfalls that will happen along the way. Inevitably, those failures will come. But, the beauty is, those failures provide us with knowledge and experience. EVERY TIME we attempt to pursue new skills, we unlock a new aspect of ourselves that has never been seen before.

How did Thomas Edison become recognized as one of America's greatest inventors? What adversity did Michael Jordan endure to become a great basketball player? The answer to both questions involved failure... and a lot of it. We can attribute failure to each step in the development process. If used correctly, failure can show you exactly what steps need to be taken to promote the highest levels of growth. More importantly, it can show you the unique gifts and talents that the world NEEDS from you. What you can uniquely give to the world creates self-worth. Furthermore, your gifts and talents, when added to the gifts and talents of people around you, create institutions teeming with pride.

WHILE IN THE FIRE, SELF-ESTEEM LOOKS LIKE....

SHORTSIGHTED FOCUS

Think more about the person you want to become or the achievements you want to earn, not just what is happening in the moment. It can be a hard thing to do, but we must focus on having the correct perspective. Your current situation is not your future situation. If you aren't happy with what is happening right now, you have the power to change it. That is one of the most beautiful things about living. You have active control over your future.

UNREALISTIC GOALS

Our self-esteem can take a lot of damage if we don't have a realistic view of our goals. Having a dream for yourself is great, but believing that will happen overnight or without effort is crazy. Unfortunately, too many young people think the work that goes into a dream is WAY LESS than the actual work needed. Find a mentor who can help you map out a plan. Then set your sights on shorter, more frequent goals on your way to stardom!

COMPARE AND DESPAIR

The invention of social media has created more self-esteem issues than anyone could have ever imagined. As a result, the creation of our second identity, which prevents others from seeing who we really are, has cursed our self-esteem. The comparison game is a total trap. You compare yourself to someone else, feel the need to post something "unreal," literally, and get a small sense of imaginary positive self-esteem. Repeat. At some point the cycle has to stop. Interrupting the pattern may require an authentic look at yourself and a willingness to press pause on social media.

WHEN SELF-ESTEEM IS FORGED, IT WILL...

EXERCISE

Few things in life give you an instantaneous sense of accomplishment like exercise. For some, exercise can feel like a burden, and for others, liberating. Regardless of your feelings about it, spend at least a few days a week exercising. There is so much research affirming the cognitive and physical benefits of strenuous work. Making a commitment to do this frequently will provide a great boost to your self-esteem.

LEARN HOW TO ACCEPT COMPLIMENTS

When you feel bad about yourself, accepting compliments can be a mental battle between self-worth and self-esteem. Am I worthy of the compliment? Was that a genuine compliment or something to make me feel better? These are some questions we ask ourselves immediately after hearing kind words. Hear the compliments for what they are and be thankful in receiving them.

HELP SOMEONE

If you are struggling with self-esteem, find someone you can help. It makes us feel amazing! Maybe you're thinking, "I don't know who to help or how to help someone." This is simply a matter of perspective! Often, we get so wrapped up in our own worlds and what is going on around us, we fail to see the needs of others. If we can shift our perspective from our own needs to the needs of others, doors will open up. Being aware of others around us, coupled with an authentic willingness to help, will naturally create a sense of gratitude and humility, both of which help our self-esteem dramatically.

5

SACRIFICE

"Great achievement is usually born of great sacrifice, and is never the result of selfishness."

— NAPOLEON HILL

WHO HAS SACRIFICED THE MOST FOR YOU IN ORDER FOR YOU TO succeed?

Sacrifice is scary. It means giving up something of value today to achieve something more valuable later. The even scarier part: there is no guarantee that the sacrifice will produce the outcome you want. Deciding to sacrifice takes guts. It means you will accept the outcome of your sacrifice no matter the end result. Although fear is associated with sacrifice, there is another important word that needs to be discussed: Hope. Hope is the driving force that propels action, and action will always produce *something*. Without hope and sacrifice, success will never happen.

"There is no success without sacrifice. We experience success because someone else sacrificed for us."
 - John Maxwell

JOHN MAXWELL IS EXACTLY RIGHT; WITHOUT A WILLINGNESS TO sacrifice, success is just a thought. Unfortunately, the idea of sacrifice is often a roadblock, causing many to refuse to start the journey toward achievement. If you were to take a moment and think about the amazing life you have, you would be unable to ignore the tremendous amount of sacrifice that thousands of people throughout history have made so that you could be where you are today. Take a moment and reflect on what others have done to put you in the position you are currently in. Think about yourself as a son/daughter, brother/sister, student, athlete, musician, artist, etc.

· · ·

Thinking about what others have given up for us can create a sense of humility and gratitude. Indeed, much has been given for all of us! We could ask a deeper question of all this sacrifice: why would someone so willingly give for our benefit? This is a complicated question that most of us don't understand until we are a little older. As a child, I heard my parents say all the time, "Do you know what we've done for you?" I, like most kids, had no answer. Now, as a parent, I understand WHY my parents asked this rhetorical question. It takes a lot of sacrifice to raise a happy and healthy family. It has taken a lot of life experience and leadership experience to understand WHY people sacrifice their wants and desires for others.

If you could, imagine two hills with a round valley in between. On one hill you are standing in your current situation or place in life. On the other is where your future self wants to be. You know that in order to get from one place to another, you must move. Here is where things get awesome! It is the sacrifices of others that help push your momentum down the hill. Think about all the time, effort, and finances they have invested into themselves over the years. Then, at some point, they made the conscious decision to give it to *you*. This incredible sacrifice no longer benefits them; they give it to you for your benefit, and it propels your momentum!

This momentum drives you closer to your future goals, but it can't take you all the way up the other hill. It's at this point that you must have total control to take over. For some, the climb will start earlier. Perhaps a lack of mentorship, life circumstances, or other causes put more responsibility on you. This is neither good nor bad; it just is. If you desire to get to the top of the hill, it is going to take courage, discipline, and your own sacrifice. And just like climbing any hill, it will be a struggle.

The climb is most difficult near the top, when you're worn down, exhausted, and wondering when it will end. For some, this moment is a turning point. Many people quit on their goals and dreams closer to the top than the bottom! During this struggle of life, it will take some crucial decision-making about your priorities and what you really want. This moment of realization will force you to evaluate your goal. Your goal is in the clouds of the summit; it will take a truly humble spirit to seek out those who can help you see through the clouds.

When you get closer to the top is when you have an epiphany! The sacrifices others have made for you and the sacrifices you have made for yourself allowed you to get to the top. All the wisdom gained through experiences, the relationships you have fostered, and the "stuff," either material or financial, you have earned can't be taken with you when you're dead. What better gift than to give it away? Just as you have been blessed by those before you, you also will help propel the next generation to reach their goals!

Do I REALLY NEED TO SACRIFICE TO FIND SUCCESS?

Yup. As mentioned earlier, sacrificing your personal wants and desires can be scary. But what is most scary is when you have to sacrifice your ego to move forward. The willingness to sacrifice your ego is called humility. It is not thinking less of yourself; rather it is thinking about yourself less. In a humbled state of mind, your true potential unfolds. Just the thought of letting go of their social status or control over what they know to be comfortable, paralyzes many people. However, when a person can listen with an open heart, learn with an open mind, and see the needs of others, everyone will benefit. It is nearly impossible to be a great teammate, parent, son/daughter, or employee when you do not possess humility.

While on your journey to developing your future self, few things are more important than humility. Humility is the foundation of teamwork and one could argue that the potential of any team, organization, or institution is determined first by each individual's willingness to embrace humility.

WHILE IN THE FIRE, SACRIFICE LOOKS LIKE....

THE NEGATIVE VOICE IN YOUR HEAD

Without a doubt, the hardest part of sacrifice is the constant battle with yourself. Have you ever noticed that your mind is constantly narrating your life? If you're like me, that narrative is processing and evaluating every decision, conversation, and event. That narration is the mind's way of trying to comprehend how the world is affecting us. There is great power in knowing that YOU actively choose how your thoughts affect you! This struggle for control of your thoughts is a lifelong challenge. However, how you think and feel about your circumstances, including when you sacrifice, is in your control.

UNDEFINED GOALS

It is really hard to give anything up if you don't know what purpose it will serve. Having clearly defined goals will help you navigate your decision making. When you know where you want to go, it becomes easier to set things aside that may prevent you from attaining your goals in the future.

A WEAK NO MUSCLE

Saying no to anything is a sacrifice. This skill is at the heart of sacrifice. In our world, there are so many distractions that keep us from becoming who we want to be! Your ability to recognize these distractions and choose to avoid them is what I call "flexing your NO muscle!" Trust me, I understand how hard it can be to live distracted; I am a seasoned professional. Remember, no great things in life are ever accomplished without sacrifice! Flex that NO muscle!

WHEN SACRIFICE IS FORGED, IT WILL...

FOCUS

Getting yourself in the right frame of mind is the most important part of sacrifice. Spending time at the beginning of every day to set your intention and remind yourself of your goals is a great way to gain momentum. Even just a few minutes can do wonders!

MAKE A LIST

It is always easier to say you're going to do something than actually doing it. Most often it is because unforeseen circumstances interfere with where you are trying to go. A helpful exercise is to make a list of potential issues you may confront on your journey and what you are going to do if and when they present themselves. This list should not only include issues from the world around you but also the thoughts you will probably hear from yourself.

SEEK ADVICE

Billions of people have lived before you. It's easy to forget that someone has probably taken the same journey that you are on right now. Asking for help is not a sign of weakness, it is a sign of humility. Finding someone who has inspired you to pursue your goals is a great way to help navigate some of the most difficult decisions you will need to make. Often when we ask these mentors for advice, they can help by sharing their experiences and providing support in times of need.

6

ACHIEVEMENT

"What you get by achieving your goals is not as important as what you become by achieving your goals."

— HENRY DAVID THOREAU

ACHIEVEMENT IS CORRELATED TO SACRIFICE.

ACHIEVEMENT IS NOT THE AVERAGE.

ACHIEVEMENT IS THE DIADEM OF EFFORT.
Diadem - a jeweled crown or headband worn as a symbol of sovereignty

WHY DOES FINISHING SOMETHING FEEL GOOD TO US?
When we make goals for ourselves, we figure out ways to achieve them. Doing so requires us to form a system (long-term goal), put in the work (short-term goal), or a combination of both. The plans we make and the work that we do inherently get us closer to reaching that goal. Achieving our goals can be tremendously rewarding. In fact, it is a primal necessity. Think about our ancestors 10,000 years ago. They weren't worried about their Snapchat streaks, their new cars, or their dream jobs. They were concerned about finding food and not getting killed in the process. When they wanted food, they had a process, worked for it, and boom! the reward of success. This process has been ingrained in us for a long time. Just like our ancestors, one of the most important outcomes to achievement is the gaining of self-confidence and an understanding that we can do things, like chasing down a wild animal and killing it!

When a goal is reached, we are proud of our achievement. However, what we are really proud of is that we proved to ourselves that we could do it! The result is wisdom, and, more-over, the establishment of effective habits. Aristotle famously said, "The greatest victory we can achieve is over self." This basically means we have the self-control to do the things we need to do more often than doing the things that we want to do.

Pride (the diadem) comes from achievement, and achievement comes from maximizing effort. The "prize" of the process is that we gain a better understanding of ourselves. We unlock parts of ourselves that have been there all along, but we only figured them out through working hard and sacrificing things along the way. We learn about who we are and how we do things. This reflection presents us with the opportunity to identify strengths within ourselves and areas that we can improve. Either way, we must sacrifice time and effort to achieve our goals or desires.

WHY DOES ACHIEVING DIFFICULT GOALS FEEL EVEN BETTER?

In your life, you will work *really* hard to achieve a goal. Perhaps you already have. In either case, there are TWO very important lessons to learn:

- You will fail
- You will sacrifice

The hard part about working towards something big is the time it requires—definitely months, but more likely, years. In these great endeavors in life, some of the most rewarding lessons we can learn come from failure and defeat. They are, after all, our greatest teachers. If we keep our minds open, failure and defeat can teach us where our shortfalls are and how we can improve. Then we try again, fail again, and learn more. It is through this process that we learn about distractions in our lives that need to be removed. Unfortunately, some of these distractions can provide a false sense of security and comfort. Again, connecting to our ancestors, think about how many failed hunts must have occurred before success happened. New strategies were formed, new weapons developed, and new food sources were needed in order to survive.

Thankfully, we live in a modern society that provides us the luxury of food; however, the work toward achievement is the same. Today, this *necessary* process of failure and sacrifice brings many people to an abrupt stop. The focus can unfortunately shift from a goal mindset to a self-preservation mindset. They stop thinking about their future and focus more on how to get out of the discomfort they are temporarily experiencing. The select few who push through the pain and discomfort of struggle are rewarded with something more than a pat on the back, a shiny trophy, or a prominent position in the company. What they *EARN* is a DEEP sense of understanding of what it takes to truly work hard for something difficult. They prove to themselves that they can do hard things, they can recover from failure, and they can sacrifice things now in order to gain something better in the future.

CAN TRUE ACHIEVEMENT <u>EVER</u> BE ACCOMPLISHED <u>ALONE</u>?

In our pursuit for achievement, there inevitably comes a point that you think "this is good enough." If you're lucky, or have people of integrity around you, you'll be told that what you've done isn't actually "good enough." Rather than being defensive, see the evaluation for what it is– a compliment. Mentors care enough to help push you even further. They help you understand that what appears to be a hill is actually a mountain. More importantly, the peaks of the mountain are in the clouds.

One of our greatest downfalls is our failure to see our true potential. Mentors are a gift! These people can see our greatness. They can push us further than we thought possible. They create more vision, show us more opportunities, and provide more inspiration to achieve greater heights. What's even more awesome is that these people oftentimes are the ones who helped us get our momentum started from the beginning.

There is a huge misconception that winds its way into our thought process after we achieve something big or small. We think, "Look at me, look at what I have done, I AM AWESOME!!!" These are tempting words, and some people actually say them. More often than not, these people are brushed to the side and ignored. The truth is that very, very, very few things in life can ever be accomplished alone. The personal sense of pride that is felt when achievement happens is real, and it is important. But if you have ever watched someone give an acceptance speech, few people ever talk about how amazing they are. Instead, they instantly give thanks to the people around them who helped them achieve. They deflect their personal achievements to incorporate family members, co-workers, teammates, and mentors into their celebration. This is genuine humility.

The biggest achievements in life should always be celebrated with others. As with our ancestral hunters, the feast is always enjoyed together!

WHILE IN THE FIRE, ACHIEVEMENT LOOKS LIKE....

MISGUIDED MOTIVES

Life is full of decisions. We make hundreds, if not thousands, of decisions every single day. Some are bigger than others, but this fundamental joy in life is not done without some risk. The pursuit of achievement can create a clouded perspective behind a very important question. WHY? The motives behind our decision making can have a significant effect on the outcome. Those who choose to pursue achievement for power, wealth, and personal gain often lead a path of destruction, harming people, institutions and organizations they come into contact with. A careful review of *why* you want to achieve is an essential part of the process. If you know why you want to do something, passion will certainly be with you along the way!

LACK OF VISION

One of the great dream killers is lack of vision. Most people think they know what they want out of life, but cannot orchestrate a plan to get it. This plan is the process. Great visionaries don't just see the top of the mountain, but they see the path that must be taken to get to the top first. If you know what you want, but aren't sure how to get there, ask someone for help!

LONELINESS

We are social beings. We crave connection and companionship. Nothing can be more detrimental to achievement than the feeling of going on your journey alone. There will definitely come a time when isolation and independence will happen, but it cannot last forever. Maybe you are saying to yourself, "It just feels like I'm doing this alone." In these moments, communication is key. If you're lonely, humble yourself and reach out to someone you know. They may have no idea you need someone to connect with.

WHEN ACHIEVEMENT IS FORGED, IT WILL...

SACRIFICE TODAY, BUT NOT FOREVER

Andy Stanley has built a great reputation as a leader and has a great practice for each season of life. Seasonally, (Monthly, Yearly, Longer) we should create a list of things that we need to set aside. He refers to this list as his "Not today, but not forever" list. What parts of my life do I need to put on hold today, but not forever? What do I need to give up today, but not forever? What actions must I take today, but not forever? This can be a powerful tool in helping us realize everything has a season. Some things are intended for today, but not forever. Creating a list of these things can help streamline your pursuit of greatness.

BE A GREAT TEAMMATE FIRST

There are plenty of works in life that require individual effort to create individual progress. However, most of what we do has a bigger implication for the group as a whole. Think of the education system. Sure, there are individuals who pursue their own personal goals. But what are they doing with their diplomas and degrees afterward? They will take what they have learned and apply it to benefit their communities, states, and nations. Life is a team game and, whether or not we realize it, all of us are working for the benefit of everyone. Being a great teammate means you are not solely focused on what's in it for you, but on a collective desire to benefit the group.

LEARN FROM THE BEST

Humility is the foundation of all great achievements.

Humble people will look at the achievements of others and apply lessons to their own lives. Here is some great advice: find someone who has modeled greatness. Clearly they have figured out a brilliant plan and have executed it well. There is plenty to learn from others, and if you ask, they are probably willing to share part, or all, of their journey with you!

PART III

DISCIPLINE

Discipline is the antidote to chaos. There are far too many distractions in our everyday life that try to pull us away from our full potential. If we don't have some control over our outcomes, we desperately search for things to control. Discipline is a skill that produces change. In the journey to self-awareness, there are few values more important than discipline.

Discipline is the war for our mind, body, and spirit. This war takes years of fighting. As most adults would openly admit, it is a constant battle, most of which happens in our own heads. The more we learn about managing ourselves and interacting with our world, the more we unlock the most powerful tool on the planet: the human mind.

Discipline of Self defines the idea of discipline and connects it with our everyday life. All of us have goals/dreams, but how do we get there? The answer lies in discipline.

Discipline of Control outlines the fundamental truth that there is very little in our lives that we can actually control. It is imperative that we recognize what we can control and let go of what we cannot control.

Discipline of Reflection is a practice that has been diminished by society. With so many distractions pulling us this way and that, taking time to reflect has become a secondary thought. In truth, nothing can offer more balance than healthy reflection.

7

DISCIPLINE OF SELF

"Self-discipline is a form of freedom. Freedom from laziness and lethargy, freedom from the expectations and demands of others, freedom from weakness, fear, and doubt. Self-discipline allows a person to feel his individuality, his inner strength, his talent. He is the master of, rather than a slave to, his thoughts and emotions."

— H.A. Dorfman

WHAT IS SELF-DISCIPLINE?

Discipline is regularly seen in a negative context by most young people. The Oxford dictionary defines it as "the practice of training people to obey rules or a code of behavior, using punishment to correct disobedience." Although discipline is an important element of any society, you are all too familiar with the idea of "do this or else". Instead, we are more interested in positive self-growth. Consequently, SELF-DISCIPLINE is going to be the center of our discussion. Self-discipline is defined by the *same* Oxford dictionary, as "the ability to control one's feelings and overcome one's weaknesses; the ability to pursue what one thinks is right despite temptations to abandon it." This is quite a different definition when the word "self" is placed in front. Personal growth is the key to becoming the person the world needs from you, and self-discipline is the key to unlocking the best version of you!

WHAT DO YOU WANT TO BE?

As a high school student, there is a nagging question that people ask constantly, a question that circulates over and over again in the back of your mind, and in most cases never has a concrete answer: *What do you want to be when you grow up?* This is a troublesome question to answer, especially for adolescent kids without a lot of life experience. There are better questions that we can ask that will give you more significance for today.

What do you want to be tomorrow?

What do you want to be by the end of the school year?

What do you want to be at this time next year?

This list of chronological questions can help guide you to some short term and long term goals for yourself. Thinking about your future is an important part of personal development. The right progression of future thought, however, is key to unlocking your full potential. Notice that these questions do not have an outcomes-based answer; they are not asking what you want to accomplish or what you will achieve. Instead, they are questions to guide your identity, who you are going TO BE. Your challenge is to take a few minutes and think about these questions. For the sake of monitoring yourself throughout the year, write down a few thoughts about who you would like TO BE by the end of this year. Remember, the results should not be an outcome, but identity-based.

Identity Example: I want TO BE a better reader.

Outcomes Example: I want to read 5 books by the end of the year.

DO YOU HAVE A PLAN TO GET WHERE YOU WANT TO GO?

When you think about modifying your identity, you must have a plan. Sticking to the plan is called SELF-DISCIPLINE. A key element to being self-disciplined is rooted in developing your identity. Having TO BE statements is critical to this development. Looking at your "to be" statements, develop a list of actionable steps that connect with what you want to be. For instance, if I want TO BE a better reader, I need to ask some questions: what do skilled readers do? How often do they read? What do they read? If I want to get into better shape: what do "fit" people do? If I want to be a better brother or sister: what does that look like?

Undoubtedly, temptations will come to challenge your identity. Being able to resist these temptations is self-discipline, and positive self-talk through these moments of temptation is a must. Having a plan in place to help form your identity is a powerful tool for positive self-growth.

Take a few minutes and devise a plan to help you solidify your TO BE statements. These questions can help:

Sharpen Your Edge

---

1. WHAT DO YOU NEED TO DO DAILY?

2. WHAT CHALLENGES WILL YOU FACE?

3. WHO CAN HELP SUPPORT YOU?

WHILE IN THE FIRE, SELF-DISCIPLINE LOOKS LIKE...

TEMPTATIONS

Becoming a disciplined person is HARD! It may be one of the greatest challenges of life. There are constant forces working to throw you off track and keep you from being disciplined. If you know that soda is a temptation, remove it from your space. Perhaps television is the culprit! Unplug it from the wall or remove it from your bedroom. There is great power in knowing your weaknesses; removing them, or at least limiting them, can have unexpected positive results.

BAD HABITS

Admit there are things limiting your potential. What would happen if you rid yourself of them for 21 days? I would be willing to bet, if you could win a 21 day battle, you could win for 22 days... then 23! Identify the bad habits that are distracting you and challenge yourself to get rid of them.

REFUSING ACCOUNTABILITY

Listen to what other people say and determine if it is valid and useful. You cannot live under the assumption that only you know best or that only others know best. Instead, listen to yourself and others, and give yourself *time* to process your thoughts.

Some people exaggerate how awesome you are, and some exaggerate how crummy you are. Rather than thinking in either extreme, focus on being disciplined in small ways on a daily basis.

WHEN SELF-DISCIPLINE IS FORGED, IT WILL...

UNDERSTAND THAT SMALL THINGS MATTER

Some people believe that in order to be disciplined, you must be in complete control of your life. Wrong! Discipline starts with the small things. If you can start small, the big things will naturally take care of themselves.

WAKE UP AND GET RIGHT TO WORK

Nothing sets your day off better than having a sense of accomplishment right away in the morning. I love the book *Make Your Bed* because it so perfectly describes that emotion! Admiral William McRaven encourages us all to wake up and make our beds the best we can in the morning for a few reasons. Most notably, it gives us a sense of pride and accomplishment before we leave our bedroom!

THINK POSITIVELY

Start saying that you are something, instead of saying you can't do something. Self-talk is a powerful tool. Speaking to yourself in the right way changes your view of yourself. Negative talk only produces negative results! Flip the script and speak like you're the champ!

8

DISCIPLINE OF CONTROL

"Happiness and freedom begin with a clear understanding of one principle: Some things are within our control and some things are not."

— EPICTETUS

WHAT IS SELF-CONTROL?

The beginning of self-discipline is self-control. Understanding the parts of our lives that we can or cannot control makes a big difference in how we view our life situations, relationships, and choices. Epictetus was a former Greek slave who was later freed and became a philosopher. Many of his writings are about "The Art of Living". In his works, Epictetus spoke about choices, distractions, friendships, and many other topics that are still relevant today. In his discussion about what we can control, he argues that our internal thoughts and beliefs are always within our control, but the view others have of us - our birthplace, our body type, etc. - will be things that l never change. Yet how much time do we spend thinking or worrying about those things?

- Why is it a bad thing to be consumed by what you cannot control?
- Who affects us most?
- What might happen when we let go of control?

WHAT THINGS IN YOUR LIFE CAN YOU CONTROL?

This might sound like a simple task, but the organization of these things is important for us to be able to move forward. Begin by listing aspects of your life that you cannot control. Included here are where you live, your current family situation, etc. Many of the things we worry or even think about the most are things we actually cannot do anything about.

Then list the things you *can* control. Your thoughts, your decisions, and your actions are all things within your control. Hopefully, two things start happening: one, you let go of the pieces of your life that you really can't change and you accept that and two, you understand that your thoughts and reactions to everything ARE within your control. You cannot control that your science test final is this week. You *can* control how you study, think about, and prepare for that exam. You cannot control what jobs your parents have, but you *can* appreciate their efforts to feed and clothe you and provide you with a place to sleep (go back to the ideas of gratitude).[1] Ultimately, this list will show you how much freedom you actually do have in your life because of all the small decisions you make daily.

- Create the lists, leave a couple of spaces to be filled in at the end.
- What understanding was gained from creating this list?

HOW CAN YOU MAKE YOURSELF MORE AWARE?

While I'm sure your list is excellent, it is nowhere near complete. As you move through the next week, take time to notice all the decisions you make in a day. Are they about things you have direct control over? Are you trying to control someone or something else? Understanding what you *do* control gives you more freedom and flexibility with how you think and act. Trying to control things that are not naturally yours leads to disappointment and frustration. Developing the self-awareness to address control in your own life and combining those ideas with self-discipline prepares you for an important part of discipline: self-reflection.

How does this awareness actually make you more self-disciplined?

WHILE IN THE FIRE, SELF-CONTROL LOOKS LIKE....

PARALYSIS BY OPINIONS

Part of our feelings of worth come from the opinions of other people. What they say about us matters. However, giving too much power to the opinions of others is supremely unhealthy. They can help guide and shape our decisions, but should never be the primary driver of our actions.

NO FOCUS

Part of the discipline of control lies within our focus. Take handwriting, for example. At some point, you had to focus on writing well so people could read your words. If you never intentionally chose to focus on having good handwriting, you probably still don't. Being self-controlled means focusing your efforts on what you're doing in each moment.

ACTING ON IMPULSE

We don't take the time to think about what we are doing and why we do it, especially when we are frustrated or angry. Our emotions (attitudes) can get the best of us if we aren't careful. When we make emotional snap judgments, we limit our ability to solve problems carefully, and we may even turn a problem into a catastrophe.

WHEN SELF-CONTROL IS FORGED, IT WILL...

UNDERSTAND THE CONSEQUENCES

Everything we do has consequences. The word consequence often has a negative association, but there are plenty of positive consequences also. A person with self-control recognizes that each controlled decision and action leads somewhere. Thinking about the consequences of an action BEFORE you act is the best practice of self-control.

START SMALL

Actively pursue one or two ways that you can practice self-control and follow through with your plan. It can be something simple, like giving up sugar for a week, sticking with a set bedtime, or spending time with someone in your family on a regular basis. Baby steps here will lead to giant strides later.

REST

We are all busy. The discipline of control takes a significant amount of brain power and action. The more self-controlled you become, the more tired you will become. Listen to your body. Rest when you need it!

9

DISCIPLINE OF REFLECTION

"Learning without thought is labour lost; thought without learning is perilous."

— CONFUCIUS

WHAT DISTRACTS ME?

A disciplined person is reflective. The problem with reflection is that we have better things to do. The world is filled with a tremendous amount of distraction, and the vast majority of those distractions are petty, self-indulgent, shallow, and are simply a "make you feel better for a minute" type of distraction. It is the world we live in, and unfortunately for you, it has blinded you from experiencing the person you can become. Somehow, companies have become experts in finding clever ways to distract you ALL THE TIME! Now you have become an expert at distracting yourself. I bet even while you're reading this, you have probably been tempted to check your phone or talk to a friend because you have been trained to protect yourself from.... you. You need to know that taking time to be quiet and have a conversation with yourself *about* yourself, is totally normal, and successful people do it all the time.

HOW DO I CREATE BETTER HABITS?

I think we can all admit that the distractions of our world have slowly drowned out our ability to reflect. At some point, you have been in a quiet place, freed from distraction and able to just think. These moments are so important for self-awareness of your emotions, strengths, weaknesses, and dreams. Without taking time to intentionally shut out the world, you are preventing yourself from finding these important values in yourself. The first challenge is to take five minutes a day and just ponder on your day, your week, and your life. In doing so, hopefully you will reconnect with the TO-BE statements you developed.

Sharpen Your Edge

THERE IS POWER IN SELF-REFLECTION! WRITING IN A REFLECTION JOURNAL CAN HELP TRACK PROGRESS YOU HAVE MADE OVER TIME. HERE ARE A FEW SIMPLE QUESTIONS TO HELP PROMPT SOME REFLECTIVE THOUGHTS DAILY AND WEEKLY.

- WHO/WHAT ARE YOU THANKFUL FOR TODAY?

- ARE YOU SATISFIED WITH MY DAY-TO-DAY ROUTINES?

- WHAT CAN YOU ADD/SUBTRACT TO MAKE MY DAYS MORE MEANINGFUL/BENEFICIAL?

- WHAT HAS BEEN THE MOST IMPORTANT THING YOU HAVE LEARNED THIS WEEK?

- WHAT <u>MUST</u> YOU GET DONE THIS WEEK?

Those to-be statements were the first level of action in becoming more disciplined. The next step is to make new habits. A good habit is started by making it obvious. If you want to be a better student, it could be as simple as placing your backpack in a place everyone will see it. If you were like me in high school, you took your backpack to your room and placed a variety of dirty clothes, blankets, and pillows over it, so Mom and Dad wouldn't ask the annoying question: "Do you have any homework?" DUH!! NOPE! What would happen if you placed your backpack in the middle of your living room? It would be pretty obvious, just sitting waiting for you to open it up and start working. Additionally, by doing so you are ALLOWING other people to hold you accountable. Your parents will be much more aware and probably ask you to move it. You pick up your bag, and BOOM, a simple reminder that you need to study for your algebra test! Make it obvious and take your first step to a better habit.

WHAT CAN YOU DO TO CREATE BETTER HABITS?

Your backpack is open, and the contents are out on the table! That's a win. It is obvious to you and those around you that this is something that is important to you and that it needs to be done.

Easy.

"Easy" is just that. Making a change in your life can and should start with something that is relatively easy. You want to be a better reader? Read more. Don't feel like reading for 30 minutes every night? Read a few pages every night. Easy. Everyone can do that. But you must DO something for this to work. Everyone can reflect on the things in their life that they would like to change, but doing something about it is the difference between happier, successful people and those who are not. Doing something fills the gap between the dream that you have or the place you want to be and where you are now.

Start small with big in mind.

The other part of making obvious and easy changes to your routine/life is making sure the people who love and support you know what you are trying to change. The environment you are in has a tremendous amount of influence on how successful you can be with your desired change. Friends and family can encourage you and hold you accountable on the days when you don't want to take those easy steps toward growing. We all need mentors and help. Surround yourself with great people who want to see you grow!

WHILE IN THE FIRE, SELF-REFLECTION LOOKS LIKE....

A CELL PHONE

If you think you can find time to sit quietly and think with your cell phone in the same room...you're only fooling yourself! There are far too many distractions and temptations on your phone. This is the biggest distraction in your life. Remove it from your space during your self-reflection time.

MR. BAD ATTITUDE

Bringing the right frame of mind to a thinking session is critical. A mind filled with anger, anxiety, or even sadness needs particular attention. Taking a few moments of controlled breathing can help calm any negative emotions and thoughts and provide a sense of much needed clarity.

NOISE

Sometimes music can take us to a calm place, and sometimes it can be a distraction. Having the TV on while successfully reflecting... almost impossible! Learn what is healthy for you and create an environment to help you get into the best mental space.

WHEN SELF-REFLECTION IS FORGED, IT WILL...

SELF-TALK

I know it may seem weird, but speaking to yourself out loud can be extremely powerful. Vocalizing your thoughts forces you to slow your brain, articulate your thinking, and hear yourself speak. If you have a goal, speaking it into existence is the first step in actively pursuing that goal. In fact, take out your TO BE statements and say them out loud right now.

SET OUT THEIR SHOES

Being prepared is a must. Some of the best advice I ever received happened when I was a young man. An old coach told me, if you are going to be prepared for a workout, set out your shoes the night before. Doing so forces yourself to be in the right mindset before you even start the activity. Self-reflection is no different. If you want to be intentional about spending time in reflection, set out your "shoes" to be ready.

FIND SPACE

Creating a personal space for time to think is important. For some, it may be their bedroom. For others, it may be in an obscure location. Thomas Edison, master inventor, had a couch in his office. Anytime he hit a mental roadblock, he would take a few minutes lying on the couch to stare at the ceiling. These break sessions produced some of the most important inventions in human history. Edison had a couch; where is your space? Find it and use it.

PART IV

KINDNESS

The value of kindness is so richly complex! At first glance, one might see kindness as an act of service for others. But looking deeper into this value, we discover that there is much more under the surface.

Kindness starts with taking care of yourself and learning how you make others feel. If used correctly, kindness will produce a host of selfless thoughts and teach you to create a system of boundaries to think and act in. Kindness promotes thoughts and actions in ways that make you more emotionally stable and enthusiastic about helping others every day and in every situation. The result: more respect for yourself and respect from others.

Minding Manners is as old as time. Understanding how our manners can affect others is a necessary topic as we pursue our quest for developing self-awareness.

Courtesy isn't just a word describing proper behavior; it's about building up your community. This section outlines the importance of courtesy and its value to your surrounding world.

Boundaries and Kindness helps lay a foundation for understanding why people act kindly. By establishing boundaries for our lives, we are able to think and act kindly within our values.

Generosity and Kindness uncovers what we actually have to give and, more importantly, why? In addition, we discuss the important distinction between giving and giving with expectation.

Integrity and Kindness brings much of what has been covered full circle. Living a life with integrity naturally produces kindness.

Respect takes time and is earned by our actions. It is one of the most important gifts we are free to give to those who earn it from us. An evaluation of the entire kindness theme is concluded with its connection to respect.The value of kindness is so richly complex! At first glance, one might see kindness as an act of service for others. But looking deeper into this value, we discover that there is much more under the surface.

10

MINDING MANNERS

"Good manners will open doors that the best education cannot."

— CLARENCE THOMAS

WE ALL WANT RESPECT. WE CRAVE RESPECT FROM OUR FRIENDS, parents, teachers, bosses, and others who are close to us. But the acquisition of respect is far more complicated than just getting a *"RESPECTED"* sticker to put on your chest. A great place to start to understand respect begins with manners. You may be thinking, "Manners are so old, no one uses manners anymore." It seems like everyone just does their thing and if other people don't like it, that's their problem, not yours. Hmmm. I think we can all agree that isn't true.

Manners, while they are sometimes annoying to hear and learn about, are one of the most important ways you can show the world you respect yourself. Manners are complicated too, so learning how manners work for you and others is an important part of your growth as a person.

What is the point of having manners?

MANNERS COME DOWN TO THIS ONE STATEMENT:

Having good manners means knowing how to handle your behavior in your life and relationships.

SO IF THAT'S NOT ENOUGH FOR YOU TO GET ON BOARD THE manners train, think about this: the most successful people have mastered their manners. If having manners means you know how to handle yourself around others, then you could imply that people with manners know how to listen, when to ask questions, and how to behave for the benefit of others. People want to be around others who have manners. Courteous people are safe, easy to work with, and bring positive energy to the work they do. It's no wonder that people who have manners are destined to be successful.

Most of us have all been learning about manners for our

entire lives! There are different social situations where manners look different. Literally hundreds of examples can be seen daily. How do I act on a bus? How do I act when walking down the street? How do I act when having a conversation? How do I act when meeting new people? The list goes on and on. Another name for all of these rules is "etiquette". For years you will learn how to act in all of these different situations, not to mention the different manners in different countries and in different cultures... yikes! Manners are the fabric of social interaction; the more you know about manners, the better equipped you will be to handle any situation.

Do I need to have manners all the time?

Manners are not like coats. You cannot put them on when you need them and take them off when you don't. As a wood-worker, I sometimes like to use stains to change the color and texture of the wood. But if the finished project is intended to be used regularly, or heavily stressed, the true color of the wood will eventually rise to the surface. The same is true of our manners. Although I want the wood to look, and even feel, differently, the true nature of the wood is always under the surface. If we expect our manners to be part of who we are, we must embrace them and make them part of us all the time!

Unfortunately, first impressions often define how people perceive who we are. Strangers don't know us like our friends know us. They aren't able to see who we really are on the inside. Instead, strangers observe our behavior and make judgments based on it. Even more, strangers make the majority of their judgments about you based on your body language. Wait! Body language has manners too? Yep! If you intend to be a person with great manners, you will need to accept the reality that you have to live with them all the time.

. . .

WHAT ARE SOME PRACTICAL MANNERS THAT EVERYONE SHOULD HAVE?

1. Smile

This could be one of the most underutilized assets of humanity. More problems could be solved and more joy could be spread if we could all learn to smile more.

2. LISTEN WITH YOUR BODY LANGUAGE

Many of us confuse listening with hearing. I can walk through my day hearing all sorts of noises, conversations, and other sounds of the world and not listen to one of them. Likewise, I can be in a conversation with someone and not listen to a single word they say. Our body language is a crucial component of listening. Try to look at the person, face them, and give non-verbal cues that you understand what they are saying (head nod). Not only is this helpful in conversation, but it's great manners also!

3. WARM GREETINGS

Saying good morning, good afternoon, or good evening are great ways to start a conversation. Speaking to people genuinely makes others feel comfortable and has an exceptional way of breaking the awkward silence.

4. KEEP IT CLEAN

Foul language is just that... foul. No one likes to be around things that smell bad. The same is true about speaking with profanity. If we are using our manners to make others feel comfortable, then having an awareness of what comes out of our mouth is extremely important. Using foul language at or near someone else will have the opposite effect.

. . .

5. COMPLIMENTS

A fantastic way to make others feel great about themselves is by giving genuine, and specific compliments. It is so easy to go through our day-to-day lives thinking only about ourselves. Acknowledging the talents and skills of others, and letting them know that you notice is the essence of manners. Not only will it make others feel good, but it will make you feel good as well!

WHILE IN THE FIRE, MANNERS LOOKS LIKE....

CONTROL

All of us want the same thing: control. In some form or another, we all strive to have control over various parts of our lives. Unfortunately, there are only a few things we can actually control: our thoughts and our actions. It is the lack of control that can spin us into a spiral of selfish thinking and acting. The result is often poor manners.

A BAD DAY

We all have bad days. The challenge is to recognize that not every day is going to be bad. If you have a bad day, bounce back and make sure that you don't have back-to-back bad days that can cause internal chaos.

LACK OF SELF-RESPECT

Respect starts with ourselves. Not having respect for yourself immediately limits your ability to think of others. Take care of yourself and you will find thinking of others becomes much easier.

WHEN MANNERS ARE FORGED, THEY ARE...

AWARE OF OTHERS

Thinking of others is the essence of manners. It starts with humility. Having a humble attitude allows us to live with great manners. Manners translate into empathy, which encourages us to understand and feel compassion toward others.

SEEKING THE POSITIVE

Everywhere we look, our world is filled with so much negativity. We are naturally drawn to see the negative in an effort to protect ourselves from it. However, when we focus too much on the negative parts of our world, we can easily be enticed into becoming a negative person. Instead, our focus should be on the silver linings of life. Be intentional about seeing the positive, and it will shine out of you like a lighthouse.

AN EXAMPLE

As social beings, we are always watching each other. If you want to see the world around you change, start by setting an example. Having great manners is contagious. When we see others with great manners, we follow suit. Make the choice to live with great manners and be a difference maker in your world.

11

COURTESY

"Talk to strangers politely... Every friend you have now was once a stranger, although not every stranger becomes a friend."

— ISRAELMORE AYIVOR

WHAT IS THE DIFFERENCE BETWEEN MANNERS AND COURTESY?

Manners are a way for you to show others you can handle yourself. Once you have an understanding of what that means, you can start to give that gift to others. Courtesy is when you apply manners toward other people. The easiest way we can understand that is through acts of compassion.

Courtesy is all about action. One cannot simply think about being courteous and do nothing. Although you may have the right attitude, your lack of action does nothing for others. Instead, there must be action in conjunction with our thoughts. Courtesy doesn't require a lot of effort; it is simply a combination of small words or actions that help others in their daily lives.

HOW DO WE SHOW COURTESY TOWARD OTHERS?

There are countless ways to show courtesy; it will all depend on the circumstance or situation you're in to know when and how to apply courtesy. Here are a few universal examples:

"Demonstrate *courtesy toward those who serve us*"

It doesn't matter who they are or what their role is, those who provide a service to us ALWAYS deserve the two most important phrases spoken around the world... Please and Thank You. Whether it is your parents, school custodians, or restaurant workers, those who go out of their way to make our lives more convenient are deserving of this simple courtesy. Furthermore, being specific about what you are thankful for adds another layer of authenticity to your words. Instead of just saying "thank you," you could be specific and say, "Thank you for holding the door open! You're so thoughtful!"

"Lend a helping hand"

When you have the self-confidence that comes from

knowing you are in control of yourself, you start to see others differently. You feel good about yourself and the world around you, so you look for opportunities to help others feel that way. One of the easiest ways to do that is to help those in need. Whether it's opening a door, picking up something someone dropped, cleaning up others' messes, or helping someone with directions, you show courtesy by doing things that will benefit everyone, not just you.

"Show up on time, and be ready to work"

Arriving on time is of utmost importance. When you make the decision to be prompt, you are telling those you are meeting that you value their time and their work. Nothing can be more frustrating or disheartening than waiting on someone. Furthermore, being ready to work is critical. If you know what is expected of you, take time to prepare yourself for the work that is necessary. Pack the essential tools, and set an alarm to ensure you are not just on time, but early. Remember, showing up right on time is like being late. Providing yourself five extra minutes, means you can unload your tools and be ready to work ON TIME.

WHAT ARE THE BENEFITS OF COURTESY?

I was walking down the street one day, and I saw a group of young people standing in a circle and talking. They were laughing and having a good time like most kids do. Out of the corner of my eye I saw a student whose backpack was unzipped; the contents of the bag were dangerously close to falling out. The student jumped up onto the curb across the street, and the backpack burst, leaving books and papers flying everywhere. The young man quickly bent over and started picking up the mess, while the wind began blowing papers in every direction. Suddenly, one of the students across the street broke from the circle and ran to help. The other kids stopped their conversation and watched as the two of them gathered the papers and got them back in his backpack. There were words exchanged between the two of them and both parted their separate ways.

This simple act of courtesy was an awesome demonstration of helping someone else. It certainly made the backpack carrier's life a little easier, and he probably felt pretty good about someone helping him out. And the student who did the helping also felt pretty good about what he did. However, the best part about courtesy is what it does for the others watching. The kids in the circle who got to witness this act of courtesy experience the same emotional connection as the other two kids. The beautiful thing about courtesy is that it does much more than just "help" someone who is in need. Courtesy creates a sense of community and connection that wouldn't otherwise exist. It propels all of us to "look out" for each other and find ways we can help!

WHILE IN THE FIRE, COURTESY LOOKS LIKE....

SARCASM

Using courteous language makes life more enjoyable for everyone. However, saying "please" or "thank you" with the wrong tone of voice can be quickly identified as fake or pacifying. If you feel like you're forced into saying thanks, perhaps it's better to say nothing at all until you are ready to be genuine.

INTERRUPTIONS

Sometimes in conversation we feel a burning desire to share our thoughts. In these moments, a rewiring of our brain needs to take place. Instead of thinking about how badly we need to say something, focus on what is being said and let the other person complete their thoughts.

CELL PHONES

The ultimate distraction: your cell phone. Believe it or not, there is common courtesy when using your phone. Looking at your phone while in conversation tells the person that you care more about who is messaging you than the person you're talking to. "But what if I'm expecting a suuuuper important text message?" If that is the case, let the person know ahead of time. Furthermore, if you are sitting at a table with someone, DON'T put your phone on the table. This is also telling the person that *if my phone buzzes,* it's more important than what you are saying. Place your phone in your pocket and check it at the appropriate time.

WHEN COURTESY IS FORGED, IT WILL...

FOLLOW THROUGH

Few things are more discourteous than not following through on what you say you're going to do. If you say you're going to meet someone at a certain time, show up early. If you promise to help a friend with a task, do it. This may seem like a simple task, but following through on your word is one of the most essential parts of being a courteous person. People are counting on you.

PICK UP AFTER THEMSELVES, AND OTHERS IF NECESSARY.

Whether it is in the classroom, bedroom, bathroom, parking lot, or cafeteria, go out of your way to make sure your space looks great! Acting in such a way builds a special level of pride to you and your community.

SAY "PLEASE" AND "THANK YOU."

Courtesy costs you nothing!

"Please," "thank you," and "I'm sorry" are the most important words you can learn to show courtesy and compassion. Use them frequently.

12

BOUNDARIES AND KINDNESS

"Compassionate people ask for what they need. They say no when they need to, and when they say yes, they mean it. They're compassionate because their boundaries keep them out of resentment."

— BRENE BROWN

WHAT ARE BOUNDARIES?

I remember sitting at the dinner table one holiday with my parents, little brother, and grandmother. I was probably 10 years old at the time, explaining how frustrated I was with my brother for something he did earlier, when the f-word hurled from my mouth. The look of pure anger and rage running through my mother's eyes pierced into my soul. My parents immediately took me to the bathroom where I experienced a mouthful of soap ...what did I learn? ...don't cuss in front of Grandma! DUH! I also learned an important lesson about boundaries and relationships that night. There are certain words that are okay to say, and other words are not. I learned clearly that night, that cursing at the dinner table, especially in front of Grandma, was a boundary you do not cross, and I still don't cross it today.

One of the lovely parts about being a social animal is learning how to interact with others. As we get older, we learn and become better at these interactions. We learn how to act in front of certain people. We learn what is acceptable to say and not say, what are appropriate behaviors, and what are not. Sometimes these lessons are learned through painful experiences, like a mouthful of soap, and others take long periods of time. Have you ever thought about why or how you learned this? Your behavior results from learning boundaries, and boundaries are an extremely important part of any relationship.

WHERE DO YOUR BOUNDARIES COME FROM?

Our world is filled with boundaries, whether you realize it or not. On the way to school today, our government set a boundary by telling you how fast you could drive to get here. The school also has boundaries: you are required to have your student ID, show up to class at a certain time, dress according to a set of boundaries, etc. On a personal level, your boundaries are defined by you but molded, to a certain extent, by others. Think about how your parents have taught you to act in front of your grandparents, their friends, or sitting in a restaurant. If you attend a church, its leaders provide a set of boundaries that are intended to provide direction for healthy interactions with God and others. Do you behave differently when you are with your friends? Chances are, the answer is yes. Why? Because your friends have a unique set of boundaries for themselves.

WHY DO BOUNDARIES MATTER?

They are common between every person, school, business, etc. that we will ever interact with. Everyone and everything has boundaries. Don't believe me, ask a rattlesnake.

Growing up in Wyoming, I had a strong sense of how to make it in "the outdoors". I didn't have to survive for a month on bugs and stream water, but had to know what to do out in the high desert. One of those things was how to deal with snakes, specifically rattlers. I've only run into a few, but they were quick to remind me when they felt threatened. That rattle is unmistakable and makes anyone nearby take notice. "Back off, or face the consequences". Rattlesnakes don't go looking for trouble, but they will provide plenty if you cross the line. We can say the same for people.

We don't have rattles that easily let others know to move along, but we all have a sense of what is okay and what is not okay. Those are boundaries. When we are young, we borrow our boundaries from the ideas of our parents, religion, schools, and community. As we grow, we should become more aware of ourselves and what influences we will allow in our lives. We eventually establish our own very personal boundaries and use them to navigate our world. The more we understand and define these boundaries, the happier we become. We learn to say yes to fewer but more important things, and no to those things that slow us down or violate our values. It's when those values are tested that our boundaries spring into action.[1]

"This is okay. This is not okay."

We have to understand and know what this means. Without a realistic view of our own boundaries, we can never see others and their boundaries. Without this skill, we are limited in the way we can be kind to one another. According to Dr. Brene Brown, the happiest and most well-rounded people she has interviewed in thousands of hours of research have been the ones who have the most well-established and defined boundaries. It's as simple as saying, "This is okay. That is not okay." Do that for yourself. Respect others when they make their values known. Work toward clear boundaries for yourself and identify the boundaries of others. This way, we can work toward the purest definition of kindness.

WHILE IN THE FIRE, BOUNDARIES LOOK LIKE....

LACKING SOCIAL AWARENESS

If we don't know how to "read the room", we make mistakes that are embarrassing to us and others. We also struggle with understanding boundaries when we don't listen to mentors when they drop the little hints of knowledge that allow us to understand how the world works. Even worse, when we don't know where to begin with boundaries, we struggle to identify what they are, much less improve upon and set them.

ROADBLOCKS INSTEAD OF ROAD SIGNS

Boundaries are in place to protect us and others. They help us all get along safely and have a common understanding of how we can all interact with each other. Instead of acknowledging the responsibility we have to our society, we see boundaries as something that limits our place in society. Seeing boundaries as roadblocks can lead to selfish actions.

MORAL AMBIGUITY

If we don't understand what is okay and what is not okay, we float between each interaction we have with the world around us. We are inconsistent with our thoughts, actions, and behaviors. People don't trust us or enjoy having us around, which is even more confusing when we don't have the awareness to understand how our actions affect others.

WHEN BOUNDARIES ARE FORGED WITH KINDNESS, THEY WILL...

PAY ATTENTION

Know what is expected of you in every situation. If you don't know or understand, look around and observe others. Ask questions of the people who have been there before. And be a quick learner. It will allow you to quickly understand how to adapt to any situation.

BE HUMBLE

View boundaries as parts of life that free you up to do what you want to do. Your understanding of the rules will give you insights into how they work and why they are there. As the saying goes, you have to know the rules before you can break them.

LIVE WITH VALUES

We learn our values from the people and institutions we are a part of. Use the best parts of those groups to sharpen your understanding of who you are and what you're all about. Then you can work on clearly communicating what those values are and what boundaries you have for yourself in relation to them. "This is okay. This is not okay."

13

GENEROSITY AND KINDNESS

"We make a living by what we get, but we make a life by what we give."

— WINSTON CHURCHILL

WHAT DOES GENEROSITY LOOK LIKE?

The idea of generosity is as old as time itself, but the actual word didn't work its way into language until the 1500s. It originally meant to be of "noble birth", or of royal blood. That might sound great to most of us, but there was a catch: to be considered generous, one had to be courageous and kind. Courage is not usually a word that we associate with generosity or kindness, but if we think about it, generosity means that we will act in a kind way with no expectation of kindness in return. It takes courage to fight the temptation to be generous and expect nothing in return. Unfortunately, this can mean some people we share our generosity with will take advantage of that kindness rather than appreciate it. When we act with kindness, we are essentially trusting in the other person with a "gift". This is why we began connecting kindness with boundaries. When we understand our values, we are more likely to trust others and be more generous with our time, money, and talent.

WHAT IS THE PURPOSE OF GENEROSITY?

Dr. Brene Brown has spent years studying human behavior. She participated in an excellent podcast with Russell Brand in June 2019. One highlight of the discussion was Dr. Brown's explanation of what generosity looks like. We encourage you to think about the following questions from the podcast:

- Do you believe, in general, that when people wake up every day, they are doing the best they can? (Usually an even split between yes and no)
- Picture someone in your life who you truly believe isn't doing the best they can.
- What if someone, who knew this person, came up to

you and said that they actually were doing their very best? Does that affect you or the other person more?

What actually happens when we assume others are not doing their best? We are mad because that other person is violating the boundaries we have for ourselves. If you lend someone money but they don't spend it in the way you think they should, you get upset. That other person didn't do what we expected them to do, and that is based on **our understanding** of the world around us. In truth, that expectation of others is usually what causes conflict within us. We get angry because people don't act in the way we believe they should. This focus on ourselves is the root of the problem. In order to understand how we can act generously, we need to refocus on our boundaries and values. Ask yourself these questions to help our transition into the next piece of generosity:

Sharpen Your Edge

---

1. WHEN WAS THE LAST TIME YOU GAVE SOMEONE YOUR TIME? WHY?

2. WHEN WAS THE LAST TIME YOU USED YOUR TALENT TO SOMEONE ELSE'S BENEFIT? WHY?

3. WHEN WAS THE LAST TIME YOU DONATED MONEY TO SOMEONE OR SOMETHING? WHY?

IS IT OK TO GIVE AND EXPECT SOMETHING IN RETURN?

The simple answer to this question..... HECK NO! If you expect anything from people while being "generous", then your definition of generosity is skewed. What you are actually creating is a barter... this for that. True generosity is given without expecting anything in return. So let's ask the obvious question, what *time, money, or talent* are you giving to the world? You may not have a ton of money, extra time, or a developed talent. That isn't the point. Being generous comes down to what you are willing to give. Should rich people give the same percentage of money as the poor? Should less busy people give more time than the busy? Give what you can. Be generous.

The struggle is knowing how and when to give generously. This is an ACTIVE choice. Being generous takes a keen focus on the world around you. If your day is fixated on your new social media posts or a "what's in it for me" mentality, being generous will be difficult for you. However, if you are actively looking for ways to give of yourself, I guarantee you will find opportunities... EVERY DAY! So let's start today. Be generous to your family. Be generous to your friends. Be generous to your teammates, if you are on a team. Be generous to a complete stranger! In doing so, you have the power to make the world a better place, one generous act at a time.

WHILE IN THE FIRE, GENEROSITY LOOKS LIKE...

SKEWED EXPECTATIONS

If you think you are doing nice deeds for others, but expect them to do something in return, you might have an incorrect understanding of generosity. People give of themselves everyday. This is their choice, not yours.

BRAGGING ABOUT YOUR GENEROSITY

Letting everyone know how awesome you are for giving a gift or doing a nice deed.... is annoying. This is a common feeling amongst most human beings. When you participate in a generous action, it's intended to make you and the person or people you are doing it for feel good. No one else needs to know.

WAITING FOR THE RIGHT MOMENT

If you are thinking about doing something generous, a trap that befalls on many people is waiting for the right time and place to do it. Unfortunately, waiting can lead to more waiting, and thus losing the opportunity to do something awesome.

WHEN GENEROSITY IS FORGED, IT WILL...

HAVE A WELCOMING PRESENCE

Many generous people have a similar character trait:they have a generous demeanor. You might be surprised by how many people you can have a positive impact on by simply smiling. Too often we are in a hurry, a neutral mood, or thinking about our dreaded responsibilities. Instead, a challenge is to think about the things you are thankful for and smile!

SEEK OPPORTUNITIES

Generosity does not have to be elaborate. There are opportunities for us to act, speak, and give generously every single day. Sometimes, all it takes is to start looking. Once you start, the doors to generous living will start opening right in front of you.

FIND A PASSION

When you have a passion, you are much more inclined to work on projects that produce joy for you. When you see that same passion in others, it can be easier to recognize great effort and great results. Acknowledging these efforts and results in others is an easy way to affirm their passion. Additionally, partnering with organizations or groups that pursue similar passions can also make it easier to generously give your time, talent, and treasure.

14

INTEGRITY AND KINDNESS

"Integrity is choosing courage over comfort; it's choosing what's right over what's fun, fast, or easy and it's practicing your values, not just professing them."

— BRENE BROWN

WHAT IS INTEGRITY AND WHY IS IT IMPORTANT?

At the beginning of this book, we discussed one of the most important values a person can wield: integrity. It is often defined as "how you act when no one is watching." But this definition only partly encompasses the full meaning of the word. We believe the other aspect of integrity is closely associated with becoming Whole or Complete. In your journey to becoming "whole", your mind-body-spirit metamorphosizes into the person you want to become. Throughout this transformation, which takes years to complete, you form your boundaries. It is within these boundaries that you act and interact with others in the ways you have established for yourself. As we discussed earlier, the more clearly your boundaries are defined, the more awareness you have to act in a kind manner. Furthermore, acting within these boundaries actually means you are acting with integrity.

But acting with integrity isn't always rainbows and butterflies. As Brene Brown says above.... it's about choosing what's right over what's fun, fast, or easy.

WHERE DO WE GET OUR INTEGRITY?

Integrity is the outward display of our values and virtues. Some of you might say "We already talked about integrity!" You are correct, but this section looks at integrity through a different lens. We first mentioned this when we talked about honor and the idea of wholeness, suiting the word to the deed, etc. This time, we are focusing on what integrity looks like in an individual person and how it is seen by others.

Our lives are filled with complexity, and the complexity of managing relationships is one of the most challenging aspects of life. We try to figure out who our "real" friends are and those who are fake. Sometimes we are the fake ones, not saying what we think or feel because we are worried about people liking us. This can lead us to do or say things we don't feel comfortable with, or that might just plain be wrong or immoral. Don't feel bad about this. There isn't a person on the planet who hasn't done this. Our goal here is to get you to understand that by being true to the values you have, you gain a sense of what integrity looks like. You won't make decisions you feel or know will compromise who you are or how you want to be perceived as a person. We develop our integrity by understanding exactly how we will make decisions before we are in those situations and limiting the chances of putting ourselves in a no-win situation.

HOW IS KINDNESS A BYPRODUCT OF INTEGRITY?

Kindness begins with ourselves. We must be able to look at ourselves and have an honest reflection about who we are and what we value. Is it honesty, friendships, wisdom, our Xbox? Regardless of where you begin, if you learn to give yourself some grace (patience and kindness) you will find that you can treat others with grace as well. Every person you meet has their own story. Furthermore, they will all teach you something, good or bad, if you pay attention to them. Kindness takes many forms, but it begins with us as a person. If we have taken the time to establish our boundaries and know what we value, we can hold ourselves and others accountable to the values we wish to live by. Kindness shows itself in the moments that integrity can be tested and presents us with yet another opportunity to grow and serve others.

WHILE IN THE FIRE, INTEGRITY LOOKS LIKE...

CHOICES DON'T MATTER

We've all had this thought: "It doesn't matter *that* much." Consequently, we say and do whatever we want in the moment. We lack the awareness that our words and actions affect more than ourselves; they affect others. This is the ultimate trap of integrity and kindness. What you say and do matters...ALL THE TIME!

EARBUDS

Listening to music is great! Could you imagine if you were on trial, and your lawyer was jamming out to Bob Marley? Chances are they would have very little understanding of what was going on in the courtroom. Like earbuds, our phones and other devices can be a distraction to our awareness of what is going on around us. Living in tune with our world means knowing when our devices are a distraction.

NO COMPASS

If you woke up tomorrow in the middle of nowhere, you would be lost. I'd bet it would take hours to even decide what direction to start moving. Living without integrity is no different. If we don't use the signs and people around us to learn and understand how we contribute to society, we end up lost. You would hop from person to person, or group to group, looking for instant acceptance, regardless of the consequences. It is no secret that this can be a very dangerous and costly way to "live." Living a life of integrity is like being in the forest with a map and compass.

WHEN INTEGRITY IS FORGED WITH KINDNESS, IT WILL...

KNOW THE IMPORTANCE OF HABITS (VIA JAMES CLEAR)

- Every action you take is a vote for the person you wish to become.

- NO SINGLE INSTANCE WILL TRANSFORM YOUR BELIEFS, BUT AS the votes build up, so does the evidence of your identity.

- HABITS ARE CRUCIAL. THEY CAST REPEATED VOTES FOR BEING A type of person.

CREATE A LIBRARY

We all need help developing and strengthening our integrity. Surround yourself with people, books, music, and ideas that promote healthy values. One of the great joys of life is figuring out what these resources are! There is more information accessible to us than ever before. All it takes is some active research and a willingness to jump in and discover the possibilities.

POINT THE NEEDLE NORTH

Understand your values and discover ways you can put them into action. Challenge your integrity in ways that are healthy. Having conversations with friends, reading challenging books, and reflecting on what you value, and why, are all ways you can point the needle north.

15

RESPECT

"Respect is for those who deserve it, not for those who demand it."

— PAULO COELHO

WHAT IS RESPECT AND IS IT EARNED OR SHOULD WE EXPECT IT?

In our society, the word "respect" has lots of definitions and uses. We are told that we should respect our parents, teachers, bosses, the President of the United States, and the list goes on and on. Why? Do we really have to? What the heck is respect, anyway? There are so many people telling us what to do, can't I just decide for myself?

Good news! Although it may seem like there is some external force telling us who and what we have to respect, ultimately, respect is ours to give freely. According to the Oxford English Dictionary, respect is "a feeling of admiration for someone or something because of their good qualities or achievements."

We get to choose who to respect and why. Think back to your priorities list developed in chapter three. You created a list of priorities that connected directly to your values. The respect we give is a direct reflection of what we value ourselves. If you value hard work, you are much more likely to respect those who work hard. If good decision-making is a priority, you respect those who make excellent decisions. Respect, however, is not something just flippantly given. In most cases, there is a very key ingredient to giving or getting respect: TIME. Earning respect takes action over time.

Sharpen Your Edge

---

1. WHO IN YOUR LIFE DO YOU RESPECT THE MOST?

2. WHAT HAVE THEY DONE CONSISTENTLY THAT HAS EARNED YOUR RESPECT?

3. IF YOU COULD MODEL ANY VALUE THAT THEY POSSES, WHAT WOULD IT BE AND WHY?

HOW DOES RESPECT FOR MYSELF AFFECT HOW OTHERS SEE ME?

Respect and self-respect allow us to structure healthy social interactions with one another. However, these two words do not have the same definition. If you were to apply the definition of RESPECT listed above to yourself —admiring yourself— we'd be talking about ego. Instead, self-respect establishes a standard for how you treat yourself and how you *ALLOW* others to treat you. This is all about boundaries.

Creating boundaries for ourselves helps us navigate difficult situations. Imagine yourself walking through a dark room. You might have a really tough time seeing where you are going, even through places you are familiar with. (Sometimes I wonder what our pets think we are doing, walking through our bedrooms and hallways like Frankenstein, trying to find obstacles on our way to the bathroom.) We have a purpose, get to the bathroom without stubbing our toes! This act of finding walls and doors paints a picture of what it is like to walk through life. Could you imagine walking in the dark without finding a wall (boundary)? You would feel lost, like you aren't getting anywhere. However, when you find a wall, it gives you a sense of security, even if you can't see clearly. Creating boundaries for your life does the same thing. Boundaries provide a sense of direction and security for you and how you live, so that you may achieve your goals. These boundaries give others a sign of how you live your life as well.

Creating boundaries for yourself and others provides a sense of awareness for how to live. This awareness is the cornerstone of self-respect. You become much more focused on what you are ok doing and what you need to say no to. The result is self-respect and respect from others.

HOW DO I EARN RESPECT FROM OTHERS?

It is important for us to understand that true respect takes time to give or to earn. Respect results from action. Although we may see someone acting in a way that we value, it takes consistency for us to give respect. The same is true about our actions. It takes consistent behavior on our part to earn the respect of others. However, the beginning of respect starts with a good first impression. Enter courtesy and manners. All people want to be treated with manners and courtesy. If you fumble through life with no awareness of those around you, chances are you're going to make some people upset. We have all been around these people. Be it fair or not, there is one word that defines them: selfish. Selfish people rarely get the respect they believe they deserve. Why? They feel like they deserve it without *earning* it.

Having manners and courtesy is the first, and a very important, step in gaining respect from others. Establishing boundaries for yourself that align with your values is next. The two of these combined make a great person! But the next, and possibly the highest, level of respect comes when you can live out your values consistently. This is arguably one of the most challenging parts of life. We all have temptations that pull us one way or another to test our boundaries. We all stumble, we all fall short, and we all fail at times. But the closer we get to living a well-disciplined life, the more respect we earn from the world. This consistency pairs perfectly with another word: Integrity, a topic we have discussed many times. Our behaviors reflect our values. Living our lives with a consistent awareness of our values is the epitome of integrity.

WHILE IN THE FIRE, RESPECT LOOKS LIKE...

A LACK OF SELF-CARE

Believe it or not, self-care is the beginning of self-respect. There are several areas in life that fall into this category. Making healthy choices about eating and exercise shows others you care for yourself. Taking pride in personal hygiene and dress also shows the world that you care for yourself. Most importantly, and sometimes most challenging, is the way you talk about yourself. Talking poorly about yourself is often a strategy to get others to have sympathy for you. Sometimes it works; however, it's more likely that negative self-talk will damage your own image and create a negative aura that nobody wants to be around.

POOR CHOICES

It takes time to garner the respect of others. Sadly, it can take far less time to damage the respect you have earned. One catastrophic decision can ruin years of work. In these moments of failure we must ask for grace. The awareness of your decision-making is paramount. After all, the respect you earn from others is not yours. They give it. Experiencing these moments is part of life. Acknowledge the mistake, learn from it, and do the best you can to move forward.

NO BOUNDARIES

Lacking boundaries for ourselves means we are pretty much willing to do anything, anytime. We call this type of person a follower. They walk through life with no direction and literally find themselves continuously in bad situations. If they are lucky, they will eventually connect with people who have boundaries. If not, the consequences of their actions, or lack of actions, will lead them down a path they don't want to be on.

WHEN RESPECT IS FORGED, IT WILL...

EXEMPLIFY THE GOLDEN RULE

Treat others the way you want to be treated. It's called the golden rule for a reason! Treating others the way you want to be treated is pure gold. This simple idea is found in nearly every culture and religion on earth. Treating others with manners and courtesy, and giving respect to those who have earned it, is exactly what we all want given to us in return.

STAND UP

Taking a stand for your beliefs can be extremely challenging. By taking action, everyone knows exactly where you stand on an issue. What can be powerful, however, is recognizing there are other eyes watching. You never know who you may inspire, who quietly agrees with you but is too scared to stand up, and who may stand up alongside you. Knowing your boundaries and fighting to maintain them is an essential part of respect.

EMBRACE CONSISTENCY

Do you want to know what really successful people do differently than everyone else? They do what they don't necessarily want to do, *consistently*. It is so much easier to lie in bed and sleep rather than wake early and get to work. It's way easier to sit on the couch and watch tv rather than exercise. Don't get me started on eating ice cream over broccoli! The most successful people in the world might make their successes look easy, but what we don't see are the little battles they win in their heads all day long. We all have them, and the vast majority of us choose the path of least resistance far too often. The select few who make the conscious choice to win these little moments are those we respect the most!

PART V

COURAGE

A gallant knight in shining armor fighting off a fire-breathing dragon is one of the first symbols I imagine when I think about courage, but I don't own shiny armor, and I've never seen a dragon. There has to be more to it.

Courage is much more than fighting a fiery beast! However, courage does require us to *fight*. The fight starts in our own minds and manifests itself into action. Courage alone isn't much; we must *do* in order to be courageous. Learning what natural abilities you have is an important part in knowing how to be more courageous. But let's get one thing straight, you won't be perfect in every moment that courage is needed.

Fight your Fear analyzes the space between action and inaction of courage. Fear can be debilitating, but even making small steps toward something that creates a personal fear takes a tremendous amount of courage. Courage is found in all parts of your life, but starts with fighting to establish your boundaries.

Talents and Aptitudes are all about our natural gifts. We live in a society where a social norm has been created to "fit in" wherever we want. A different question would more appropriately be: How does the world fit into us? It takes courage to figure out how to do this and where to go once we find out.

Fail your way to Greatness seems like an oxymoron. Throughout history, the most unlikely heroes are born because of their willingness to take the first step. Courage is simply more than a word; it requires action. Failure is just part of the process, and you cannot be afraid of it. The willingness to fail manifests into courage and, surprisingly, motivates courage in others, as well.

16

FIGHT YOUR FEAR

"He who is not everyday conquering some fear has not learned the secret of life."

— RALPH WALD EMERSON

HOW DO SUPERHEROES REALIZE THEY HAVE SUPER POWERS?

Superheroes are AWESOME! Each superhero has a story, a cause, and a drive that all of us can connect with in one way or another. However, the difference between us "commoners" and the superhero is, of course, their superpowers. But have you noticed that each superhero's story always starts with an obstacle or enemy that seems impossible to defeat? The hero struggles, almost loses, then somehow finds a way to overcome. As their story is unfolding, we fail to realize that the hero is faced with the perfect level of adversity that he/she can handle. Through their stories, we can celebrate their victories and find inspiration that can be applied to our lives.

Although these superheroes have abilities that we only wish could exist in real life, there is a common power between the superhero and us: The COURAGE to face adversity. Our story is no different from the story of the superhero. Just as they are faced with the perfect level of adversity, so are we in the quest to overcome! We are never given more than we can handle. The willingness to face your challenges is called courage, and having courage is a choice we all get to make!

ARE THERE DIFFERENT TYPES OF COURAGE?

It is easy to fall into a trap by thinking courage is achieving the superhero status by performing larger-than-life works. Although rescuing your hamster from a burning building takes courage, it is not the only way to demonstrate your courage. Courage is not common. What makes courage unique is its application. It must be connected with another value. Think about the discussion about kindness and boundaries. In order to act kindly, we must first establish boundaries with ourselves and others. When we know what those boundaries are, it is easier to act with kindness. These boundaries are important for more than just kindness. Anytime you face a struggle or a challenge, the decision to fight for your values takes courage. If loyalty is a value, then you make decisions that align with your loyalties. When our values are tested or challenged, it is COURAGE that reinforces what we value the most.

As you live from day to day, there are several areas of your life that will be tested. Social, intellectual, physical, emotional, and spiritual challenges all require courage for growth. So, what prevents us from acting with courage? Why do we act cowardly sometimes? A possible answer lies in the fear of not succeeding or getting the result we want.

REGRETS OR REGERTS?

When I think of regret, I'm reminded of the commercial with the guy getting a tattoo that is supposed to say "No Regrets," but the tattoo artist misspelled regrets as regerts. Whoopsie! The irony of the commercial fits our discussion well.

Think about something you regret not doing; going to a concert, taking a trip, applying for that job, etc. Why didn't you go for it? Many times those choices are made for us by our schedule, our income, or other factors. But other times, it is purely our decision. What things hold you back? What are you fearful of in that moment of decision? Think about personal examples where the outcome would have been something fun and positive for you to experience. "Inventory" what thoughts and feelings you had at that moment of decision. We call that moment "Crossing the Threshold". Here's what we mean:

In every great story or movie, we see the main character forced to make a decision early on, a decision that leads to a new place, relationship, dimension, who knows! What matters at that moment is that the heroes first step into what becomes a whole new world for them. They don't know it yet, but everything that has happened in their lives has prepared them for this very moment. So when that moment arrives for you, don't hesitate!

WHILE IN THE FIRE, FIGHTING YOUR FEAR LOOKS LIKE...

NEVER TAKING THE FIRST STEP

Heroes and common-folk alike never become the better version of themselves when they cannot move forward into an uncomfortable situation. We defer opportunities to others, don't step up when there's an opportunity to learn, and watch life pass us by. We never become who we were designed to be!

NOT HAVING SOMETHING TO FIGHT FOR

We don't acknowledge that we actually do care. About anything. We shrink back when our values are tested, rather than believing in ourselves and all of those pieces of the puzzle that were put together to make us who we are.

FEAR OF LOSING WINS

Better to have never fought and be safe than ever risk losing or being viewed as a failure. As heartbreaking as this saying is, we have all thought it and believed it was the better option. What a tragedy! We usually see the consequences of our actions negatively, ensuring that we will do nothing rather than something, sometimes even anything. As John A. Shedd said, "A ship in the harbor is safe, but that's not what ships are built for."

WHEN FIGHTING YOUR FEAR, COURAGE IS FORGED BY...

SAYING YES

Find ways to accept responsibility or take on a project or leadership role. It doesn't have to be big or overwhelming, it just matters that you move. We have the "equipment" we need in order to begin our journey, and we will gain more along the way. The first step is the most important one we take.

WEARING IT ON YOUR SLEEVE

It is okay for people to know that you care. Find your people, your values, your "cause," and act in ways that people clearly understand. Challenges to our values expose our courage. The more we really care about ourselves and others, the more courage we show when the moment is upon us.

KNOWING FAILURE ISN'T THE END

The closer we get to possibly achieving something, the more we become concerned about the outcome. It is in this moment that we understand that the process that led you to this point is more important than the end result. It will give you the tools you need to try again in a different way, win or lose! The only way you really lose is to never play.

17

TALENT AND APTITUDE

"We each harbour a talent. It hibernates within us, snug yet eager, waiting for the first darling buds of opportunity to emerge."

— KEVIN ANSBRO

I WAS A SENIOR IN HIGH SCHOOL; I HAD JUST SIGNED MY LETTER OF intent to play college football and was filled with excitement about the next chapter of my life. As I shared my future with teachers, friends, and family, I was peppered with the same question over and over— "What's going to be your major?" Honestly, I was so excited about playing football, I didn't have a solid answer. Consequently, I sold myself on being undecided.

Over spring break, my family traveled one last time to visit my grandparents in Lincoln, Nebraska. After our warm greetings, my grandfather pulled me aside and handed me a newspaper clipping from *The Wall Street Journal* entitled: "The top projected jobs of the 2000s". As I sorted through the list, my eyes fixed on the far right column titled "Annual Salary." Well, this is easy, I thought. I went straight to the top of the list— Computer Science. I liked computers, I understood most software, and I liked playing PC games. It seemed like a no brainer choice. What I didn't realize at the time was how much math expertise was needed in that field. Needless to say, after two years of struggling through a host of high-level math and computer programming classes, I realized that computer science sparked ZERO passion in my being... I was simply there for the money.

Looking back, I wish someone would have asked a different question. A question that tapped into understanding my natural abilities. What are you REALLY good at? I don't know if I could have answered that at the time, but I do believe it would have made me think on a deeper level.

The great temptation we all face when choosing a career can be chasing a dollar amount. In fact, my story is not different from millions of adults around the world who choose to pursue a career in something they might not actually care about. Take a moment to think: do you have any aptitudes (a natural ability or skill)?

. . .

HOW DOES COURAGE LEAD TO SELF-DISCOVERY?

We live in the greatest country in the world. There is so much opportunity for every person to learn, grow, and foster knowledge that kids around the world would be jealous. Think about it for a second: could you imagine the Pharaoh of Egypt flying to China? What about Alexander the Great having all the books in a library on a tablet? How about your great-great-grandparents having a video chat with someone across the world? Don't fool yourself; we have it made!

The best part of the American education system is the variety of skills you can learn. There is an unspoken idea that YOU have the power to choose your path to find your natural aptitudes.

Sitting through years of registration, I cringe every time one of my students asks, "What is an easy class I can take next year?" I'm not mad about the fact that they are looking for the easy way out... AKA laziness. I get frustrated about a missed opportunity. If you are serious about finding what you are naturally good at, there must be a commitment to learning what your aptitudes are. How do you know what they are? What are you doing to find them? The American school system has mastered providing this opportunity to all learners. However, you will never know if you don't try new things. Instead of running from challenges, embrace them.

So many people are afraid of what might happen if they try something new and fail. The willingness to try, even with failure as an option, is a perfect example of courage. As Les Brown says very well:

"If you want to become a person you have never been, you must do things you have never done!"

A dear friend of mine is an unbelievable baker. She didn't

go to culinary school; in fact, she couldn't even get into a cooking class in high school. Determined, she took to YouTube as her teacher. Years later, I can undoubtedly say that she contends with the best bakers around! Few things can rival curiosity and a determined spirit. We live in an age of information, and knowledge is readily available to us all the time. Learning a new skill is more accessible than any time in history. You can learn to rebuild an engine, fly fish, carve a wooden duck, or bake through a variety of media. What are you curious to learn, and what are you waiting for?

Sharpen Your Edge

___

1. WHAT SKILL DO YOU WISH YOU COULD POSSESS?

2. WHAT PLATFORM COULD YOU USE TO HELP LEARN THAT SKILL?

3. IF THERE WERE NO LIMITATIONS TO WHAT YOU COULD DO, HOW FAR WOULD YOU TAKE IT?

___

WHAT CAN YOU GIVE BACK TO THE WORLD?

What if you're the next Pablo Picasso, and you just don't realize it yet. Or perhaps you have the newest car design locked away somewhere deep in your brain. Taking a chance to find the answer to these questions takes COURAGE. At some point, you're going to have to learn what you are born to do. The journey to self-discovery can be a long, difficult one and some might say, "What if I'm not good at this or that?" or "What if you don't succeed?" So what! At least you'll know, then you can move on! Don't miss out on an opportunity to learn more about yourself. Each new piece of knowledge unlocks a new piece of you. Ultimately, you have to find your natural gifts, and the world is waiting for you to share it!

While in the fire, Talent and Aptitude look like...

EGO

Nobody likes to fall flat on their face. It's embarrassing and uncomfortable, especially living in a world that is filled with unrealistic social media expectations. Dissecting the idea of failure can be traced back to one common denominator: ego. If you think deeply about what you are really afraid of, you would probably start thinking about how others perceive you. The unwillingness to try is more egotistical than being ultra successful and bragging about it. Fighting the pressure from others is an arduous task. Shifting this focus is not only freeing, but immensely beneficial to your own development as a person.

FEAR OF SUCCESS

To be good at anything takes time and effort. Many people are afraid of these two variables on the path to success. There is discomfort in learning, but there is no need to fear becoming better. The work you put into anything will undoubtedly shine in other areas of your life.

FOCUSING ON WHAT YOU CANNOT CONTROL

There are plenty of distractions that impede personal growth. Focusing on what you cannot control is unnecessary and unproductive. Things like your birthplace, your parents, your teachers, and even your reputation are all out of your control. Focusing on your attitude, the effort you put into your work, and the dreams you have for your future should be the focus.

When Talent and Aptitude is forged, it will...

Let it rip

There are so many new things you could try to improve. The hardest part of this entire process is taking the first step! Start small on something that might not take as much time or effort. Then as you get more comfortable, take it a little farther, then push a little harder. What are you waiting for? Go get it!

Put in the time

No matter what you choose to pursue, it will take time. Nothing in this world that is meaningful and beneficial is easy to master. Masters have organized their days to ensure they are spending adequate time practicing and refining their skills. Look at your calendar and make sure you are scheduling your priorities.

Find others like them

Linking with others who share similar talents makes the development process easier. Life was not meant to be lived alone. Working together can bend the curve of development to your advantage. Additionally, you will learn tips and tricks others have mastered and you will be able to share the same.

18

FAIL YOUR WAY TO GREATNESS

"It is not over until you win"

— LES BROWN

THERE HAVE BEEN MORE THAN A FEW TIMES THAT I HAVE BEEN criticized for being a person who has very high expectations for others. I'm not sure if it's one of those things that just happens when you're a teacher/coach, but that, in fact, is very true about me. I expect your best. Every time. I am well aware that this can cause issues for some people. But I can guarantee that it has caused the most issues for me.

As a person who believes in high expectations wholeheart-edly, when it comes to applying it to myself, it can be a tremendous hindrance. If I cannot do something to the absolute best of my ability, I won't do it. That's it. I'm not good at painting the walls in the house? I won't do it myself, but I sure can save up and have someone else who is better than me do it. Have a report to make or something to type up? If it's not perfect, I'll keep putting it off just because I don't think it will ever be good enough.

I cannot tell you how many times that idea has been a negative for me or has cost me opportunities. And until I understood how I applied that to myself, I was continually engineering myself small, or in other words, underestimating my potential. My wife was the one who finally said, "Sometimes it is more important to get it done than it is for it to be perfect." She was right! I want to do my best all the time, but it's way more important to complete the task at hand than it is for it to be perfectly done. By refusing to do it unless it was perfect, I ensured things would never be done at all. When you are starving, having something to eat immediately is much more important than taking the time to make the perfect meal. Such is the way with most things in life.

Now I use that character trait to my advantage. I know which tasks just need to be completed and which ones need to be the best work I can produce.

· · ·

COURAGE IS A VERB?

I would bet most people think of courage as an effect, not a cause. We see courage in people who do things that are new, difficult, and even dangerous. But we also usually view that courage through the rearview mirror, noticing how courageous someone was at that moment in time. Or we consider courage as a value or virtuous thing that only a few of us possess, and it certainly is, but we would like to take a unique approach toward courage, and how it gets us from good to great.

Instead of courage being a way we describe choices and behavior, we are using courage as a verb. Now we know that we cannot change the descriptor of what a word is, but we are going to twist it just a little to encourage you to think in a different way. Think of courage as an action. It is a moment that requires you to do something, ESPECIALLY when there are reasons you don't want to do it. Facing your fears is the definition of courage, but actually facing them is a choice to take action! What does this have to do with greatness?

The greatest people we know, whether personally or from a book or movie, have all demonstrated that they will attempt greatness. More importantly, they do so again and again, not quitting until they reach their goal. What's even better about embracing the idea of courage being a verb is that once it happens, it never stops. You will always look for the opportunity to challenge yourself, learn from your mistakes, dust yourself off, and go for it again. Going for it is what courage is all about. It really is the working definition of failing your way to greatness! (Even better, we can find many ways to be courageous; spiritually, emotionally, physically, etc.) Most importantly, it gives us what we need to try against the most insurmountable odds, when there appears to be no chance to come out victorious. Remember, we find the victory in the effort, not in the result.

. . .

HOW DOES COURAGE BECOME BRAVERY?

Now what? I continue to fail my way through my fears and am ready to face new challenges, but what is the end goal here? Why does this matter?

As we continue on our journey of personal growth, we will continue to answer this question in a similar fashion. The true test of a virtue, value, or characteristic is not how it benefits you. Rather, it is when that trait becomes a source of strength for others that it comes full circle.

Bravery is the next level of courage. Bravery takes that fear that we used to have, places it aside, and pushes us to the next challenge. It is important for us to feel, but even more important for people to see. Bravery inspires others to be courageous or brave themselves. Some of the greatest leaders we have ever known demonstrated bravery on countless occasions. Even more importantly, they usually have the insight to use that bravery when it matters most.

Sharpen Your Edge

1. WHO ARE LEADERS THAT HAVE DEMONSTRATED BRAVERY?

2. WHAT DID THEY DO TO EXEMPLIFY BRAVERY?

When we use bravery in our own lives, we open up doors for our future and find out that we are capable of more. When others see that bravery, we inspire that same resilient spirit in them. Bravery is the gift we can give to others and pave the way to greatness in the process.

WHILE IN THE FIRE, GREATNESS LOOKS LIKE...

PERFECTIONISM

Good is the enemy of great. Perfectionism is the enemy of finishing tasks. Instead of focusing on the process and how things can get done, and getting them done, we worry if it's good enough. Even worse, we convince ourselves that it will NEVER be good enough, and therefore it is not worth the effort.

LACK OF FAITH

Accomplishment is fun! But instead of focusing on what could be, we concentrate on the horrible things in our heads that will most assuredly happen if we even try. We allow our negative thoughts to dominate our self-discussions, limiting our opportunities and our chances of envisioning a brighter future.

A SOLO FLIGHT

Rather than surround ourselves with people who recognize the great potential in us, we choose to go it alone. In doing so, we forgo important insight and direction we might get from those closest to us.

When Greatness is forged, it will...

Answer the Call!

Go for it! When the opportunity for greatness presents itself, you have already done everything that you needed to do. You're ready. It doesn't guarantee that you will get the result you believe you should, but my goodness, will you become something great along the way!

Take action!

Jump in and learn how to swim. It's not called knowing; it's called learning. The only way we learn is by beginning, failing, correcting, and failing again. Process over product.

Circle the wagons

Welcome people into this part of your life that will be honest and encouraging. Seek out mentorship from those who you believe to have similar values and ethics to yours, and who will use their knowledge and experience for your benefit. They are fulfilling their purpose through your experience!

PART VI

UNITY

Unity is an odd concept when it comes to human beings. It's something that we don't know we were missing until we achieve it, and then it becomes an obsession. And perhaps it's been there all along. We find all kinds of groups to be a part of; clubs, bands, teams, group texts, churches, etc. It's almost like everyone has the same internal drive to find others that share our beliefs and passions. But would you also agree that many, many people struggle to find even one or two other people who are like them, moreover five to ten people? There's no way there are more than twenty people like me, are there?

Truth is, there are. We just have to know ourselves and our closest allies. When we trust all involved, we will venture out to find those who are like us and form a larger band. Just as each value before, there are specific steps we must take to achieve the pinnacle of collective achievement: unity.

The One details how we become someone who understands their value as an individual. It is a bit tricky, but considering the work you have done to get to this point, it should serve as a gentle reminder of how you become the best version of you. You are immensely important to the next piece, which is the unit.

The Unit takes **The One** and puts it together with a common purpose. We will spend most of our lives in small units of five to ten people. Our ability to bring our positive attributes to the unit and recognize the talents of others will push the group to new heights. Accountability, sacrifice, and work ethic all push the unit to the precipice of greatness. When these units combine, they become the team.

The Team becomes the physical embodiment of each one and unit. They act and move as a highly complicated and capable entity. Teams make and break their own momentum, and in turn, their destiny. Teams are the epitome of human cooperation and interconnectedness.

19

THE ONE

"Good teams become great ones when the members trust each other enough to surrender the Me for the We."

— PHIL JACKSON

WHAT IS THE MOST IMPORTANT CHARACTERISTIC/VALUE YOU CAN bring to a team?

"E Pluribus Unum" is a Latin phrase we have all seen on our American currency. It is the traditional American motto, and we translate it to "Out of many, one." It is a perfect reference to the value of Unity. In life, whether or not you are an athlete, you will serve on several teams. In fact, you are part of several right now! Your family, your school, your work, and your church are all teams that include you as a teammate. So what's the big whoop, you might ask? Well, like every working group, the most effective teams are those that have a tight sense of unity. Unity means that all parts of the team are working together for a common goal or a common purpose. The better you know how to fit into the team and do your part, the more valued you will feel as a teammate, and the healthier the team will be because of you.

As you think about the question above, there are several important characteristics that you bring to a team. Hard work, loyalty, compassion, and integrity are all important. But what if those values have the wrong motive?

What if you are a crazy hard worker, but it's only for what you want?

What if you are loyal or compassionate, but it's only toward most and not all?

What if you have integrity, but only in what you want?

These are all important characteristics, but without humility, they mean little. Humility means putting your own wants and desires second to the team. It means that ALL members of your team are just as important as you. It means that you have to do what is in the best interest of the team, ALL THE TIME. Without humility, teams fall apart and usually form factions.

A faction is a fancy word for a group that causes conflict within a larger group.

When you think about the best "teams" you have ever served on, these factions don't really exist. The worst teams are those filled with selfish, "me first"- minded people who usually form nasty groups of trash talkers.

The best way we can form elite teams is for each member of the team to look inward first. You must have a humble spirit, which includes sacrificing your wants and desires, if you want to contribute your maximum to the team.

Sharpen Your Edge

---

1. WHAT GROUP OF PEOPLE IS THE BEST TEAM YOU HAVE EVER BEEN A PART OF?

2. WHAT MADE THEM GREAT?

3. WHAT HAPPENS TO THE TEAM WHEN INDIVIDUALS DON'T FULFILL THEIR RESPONSIBILITIES?

DO THE WORDS WE USE REALLY MATTER?

Interacting with our teammates can bring a deep sense of purpose and unity to our teams. If you think about your "team" of classmates or family members, how do you speak to one another? Do you share words of encouragement? Do you poke fun at each other with sarcasm or hurtful talk? The words we use with each other matter more than you might think. Although playful sarcasm can produce a few laughs, it can and will frequently produce resentment and hurt feelings. This is especially true when it happens from adults to children. Regardless of intent, sarcasm can cause a deep division in relationships and teams. Speaking words that are affirming and positive produce nothing but good for the group. Coach, author, and mentor Rod Olsen uses the acronym T.H.I.N.K. to help filter the unnecessary words when speaking to one another.

T - True

H - Helpful

I - Inspiring

N -Necessary

K - Kind

While talking with your teammates, are your words True? Helpful? Inspiring? Necessary? Kind? When speaking to one another, remember to always T.H.I.N.K before you speak!

HOW DO YOUR ACTIONS AFFECT THE TEAM?

Your teammates rely on you. We all play a role on the various teams we are on, and our actions within the team matter. Outside of completing the basic duties on the team, what are you doing to help your teammates around you?

HERE ARE A FEW THINGS THAT GREAT TEAMMATES DO:

- **Take responsibility and don't make excuses:** It is really easy to play the blame game, especially when things are not going the way you want them to. Instead, you must humble yourself and test your role in the situation. Take responsibility for your mistakes, acknowledge that you need to fix them, then make the required changes.

- **Put in the most time with maximum effort:**
  Inspiring teammates are always the ones who will go
  above and beyond in both time and effort. It is really
  hard to function as a successful team when the
  members are not willing to do their best or put in
  the necessary time into the process.
- **Humble themselves and push through adversity:**
  Great teammates are not "know-it-alls." In fact, they
  are the ones who would be the first to admit that
  there is much more to learn in order to be better,
  especially when times get tough. Adversity and
  struggle will undoubtedly happen. Being a great
  teammate means you will fight through the struggle
  and motivate teammates to keep fighting for the
  common goal.

WHILE IN THE FIRE, "THE ONE" LOOKS LIKE...

PRIDE

You know it all. No one can tell you anything. You offer excuses in defense of your prior choices rather than listen for ways to improve your future actions. Convinced you are already the best, there's no reason to listen or improve. It is a closed mindset.

DISHONESTY

When you aren't honest with yourself, you cannot be honest with others. When we don't act and speak truthfully, we will lie and blame our way out of any personal accountability.

"THE CANCER"

The primary focus is only on what **you** can get out of any situation. You bring nothing to the table, only looking for the most glory and praise, expecting nothing from yourself. You are jealous of others on the team and see everyone as an enemy or not worthy of your time and effort.

When "The One" is forged, it will...

Humble itself

Be the best learner. Soak it all in. Don't make excuses for what you have or haven't done. Listen for ways to fix your mistakes in the future.

T.H.I.N.K.

Speak with purpose and integrity. Be the person who everyone knows will tell the truth. Be intentional with what you say, who you say it to, and why you say it.

Buy in

Do it for the team. Your efforts are meaningless unless they contribute to the success of others. Celebrate the achievements of your teammates. Work harder than anyone else. Compete to the best of your ability. A rising tide lifts all boats.

20

THE UNIT

"Without trust, you're not going to be able to do much of anything. With trust, you can accomplish more than you can even imagine"

— JOSHUA PERRY

HOW DOES THE "ONE" BECOME PART OF A COHESIVE UNIT?

Units are small groups of "ones". Usually made up of a group of four to twelve people, units are one of the most common social and professional groupings that human beings have. As an individual, you can only go so far. To become better than you are today, include people in your small group, or unit, to achieve more. Current business leaders identify teamwork and the ability to work with others as some of the top priorities in their hiring practices. NFL teams are making a habit of only drafting players who were selected as team captains. Those players have already demonstrated the characteristics of moral and ethical individuals. Because of their efforts and the way they treat their teammates, these players were selected to lead their respective units. When those leaders form and lead a team together, they have the potential to form very cohesive units. But what exactly does that mean?

Cohesiveness has a few excellent variations of its meaning, and the first word that comes to mind is unity. There's that uni- again! Becoming one entity results from cohesion. Another outstanding example is found in the definition of cohesion as it pertains to physics: "... of or relating to the molecular force within a body or substance acting to unite its parts." For our understanding of the unit and its cohesion, we are going to use the second example. A force that unites individual parts into one whole. What is the force that builds cohesion and unites the *ones* into *one*?

Trust.

Simply put, when individual members of a unit trust each other, they will respect and count on each other to contribute to the best of their ability. Each individual is prepared, they communicate well, and they never act in a way that would cause their teammates to doubt their intent or commitment to the group. "You can push only to the level of trust you have built with each other" (Meyer, 2015). Groups that build trust in each other the most achieve the most. They are the most unified. It's that simple. How do we build trust with others in our unit?

HOW DOES PATIENCE LEAD TO POWER?

Everyone starts somewhere. Some people are born with incredible talent; others an equally valuable work ethic. These skills and traits can be discovered early in life, or as we reach adulthood, but unfortunately, sometimes they are never found.

When we talk about the concept of a unit, we have to begin by knowing where the starting line is for each person in the group. One member might be much further down the "leadership" line than the teammate who is more emotionally mature. Sometimes it comes down to experience; sometimes it has more to do with being in tune with the current trends. Each part of the team has to find their role and play their part for the unit to be successful.

Building the individuals within the unit while also increasing the overall performance of the unit is no small task. Achieving on the highest level requires each member to maximize their contribution to the group, while also being willing to sacrifice for the betterment of the group.

There are two important parts of each individual that will determine how high the unit can fly.

The first aspect is ego. Is every individual capable of hearing that they are good, but need to be better? Can they watch others succeed and grow without jealousy? Will they take criticism and make it constructive? Personal pride can impede many achievements. Even worse, it can be the poison that erodes the foundation of the group.

The second aspect is patience. Each person in the team will

progress at a different rate. Will those that are further ahead continue to work to their full potential while also bringing their teammates along? Patience leads to the greatest achievements. "Trust the process" is a well-used phrase, and for good reason. Group members who trust their abilities will be patient with themselves as they grow. Even more importantly, they can see the development of their teammates at their own pace.

The power of patience comes in the observation of improvement. The pace of improvement isn't as important as the consistency of the progress.

WHAT DO WE DO WHEN OUR UNIT IS TESTED?

Why are so many people afraid of speaking in public? Why do kids not try out for the school musical or basketball team? [1]They are simply afraid to fail. "You can't fail if you don't try, right?" Wrong. When that fear of failing holds us back, we fail anyway. That's why individual sports and activities are so difficult. There's no one to share the blame with. So how do the same teams or people continually amaze us with their thoughts and abilities? Behind the scenes, they have built an amazing trust and patience with their "unit," allowing them to move forward with confidence and enjoy their own performance.

Two things happen to the people in tight-knit units. They learn how to hide their fear while sharing their strength. Each person in that unit is different. They have their own fears and anxieties, but for the benefit of the unit, they push those fears aside. They know that the other people around them are there to support their efforts and won't leave them behind, regardless of the outcome. When that happens, each member of the unit becomes a leader, depending on the scenario and what they are capable of doing. By pushing doubt aside and encouraging others, even if you aren't feeling confident in yourself, you maintain the cohesiveness of the unit. You maintain trust, and patience, and the process ensues. The greatest human achievements are a result of these cohesive units.

Units maximize the talents and aptitudes of the individuals to contribute to the overall performance of the group. Symphonies know when they have aced a performance because each section of instruments performed their best. Teams know they can celebrate as the clock winds down and they are champions because each unit within that team performed to the best of their ability. The foundation of the United States was built on the cohesiveness of units from 13 different colonies. Imagine the trust and patience they had in and with each other. The unit leads to unity, the greatest collective force humans can create.

WHILE IN THE FIRE, "THE UNIT" LOOKS LIKE...

SELFISH AMBITION

There is no greater team killer than selfishness. In fact, when selfish ambition finds its way into a unit, it is impossible to reach the full potential of the group. Think of a time when you worked with someone who was inconsiderate and selfish. How well did you work together? Were you able to reach your full potential?

REFUSING TO ACCEPT FEEDBACK

One of the most challenging parts of working with people is communication. Not so much the day to day "how's it going" communication, but the conversations that deal with how to improve. It is essential to talk about how to improve process, output, effort, etc. The difficulty is, most people take these conversations like personal attacks, rather than opportunities to improve.

DISORGANIZED EFFORT

Sometimes a unit fails because the members of the unit don't know exactly what to do. Clear roles and responsibilities are a must if you want to excel. However, don't expect this to be a simple task. Oftentimes, people's best "roles" are those that are outside of what they think they can do.

NOT KNOWING YOUR PEOPLE

Getting to know the people in your unit creates a sense of belonging and camaraderie that make working together more enjoyable and fulfilling. When you don't know your people, it's much easier for everyone to "hide" in their work and remain on the fringes of good unit chemistry. The lack of relational depth limits trust, accountability, and, ultimately, your potential. Take time to ask questions about other's personal life to start growing together.

WHEN "THE UNIT" IS FORGED, IT WILL...

CELEBRATE SUCCESS

Success can look like a variety of things. It could be a win in a sporting event, a great academic performance, or even giving great effort toward any goal. In all of these instances you should be intentionally recognizing this great work. This celebration does not need to be an elaborate party or ceremony. Instead, take a moment to give specific, genuine praise for a job well done!

TRUST THAT FAILURE ISN'T FATAL

In most cases, losing won't kill you... thankfully. Instead, failure is the greatest teaching tool we possess. As mentioned earlier, most people are terrified of failure, whether they want to admit it or not. Newsflash: everyone fails, even people who are the absolute best at what they do have failed and are going to fail again. Greatness sees past failure as a personal assault and puts it in perspective. To say it another way, it's how you respond to the failure that will define who you are and what you will become.

REMEMBER THAT PATIENCE IS A VIRTUE

Rome wasn't built in a day, and neither were you or I. We must allow ourselves and others to develop over time. We live in a world that has made life more convenient, more efficient, and more streamlined than ever before. Because of this, many people think our development needs to operate the same way. WRONG! Nothing could be further from the truth. Instead, we must be willing to wait patiently for others to work through their own issues while celebrating their successes along the way.

21

THE TEAM

"For the strength of the pack is the wolf, and the strength of the wolf is the pack."

— "THE JUNGLE BOOK," RUDYARD KIPLING

DO YOU KNOW THE COMMON GOAL/VISION OF YOUR TEAM?

The single most important element to creating a unified team or group is understanding what the common goal or vision is. If you think about what this might be for your various teams, could you recite them? Chances are, if you don't know what the vision is for your team, then there is probably a lot of uncertainty and guesswork about what to do. This, of course, leads to a complete lack of unity. On the contrary, teams that know and share a common goal or similar vision propel themselves into greatness. The feelings of closeness and oneness are so strong that they will remain with you for a lifetime. It is these feelings that your parents, teachers, pastors, and coaches want to help establish in their teams.

If you want to function as a high-level team, look at this list and evaluate which parts need strengthened.

I CAN/DO:

1. Know the common goal/vision
2. Take responsibility toward achieving the goal
3. Contribute to the goal
4. Help others understand the goal

WHAT HAPPENS WHEN ALL TEAM MEMBERS WORK TOGETHER?

One of the most amazing experiences a person can have while working with a high-functioning team is growth. Elite teams are like well-oiled machines! Machines are one of our greatest achievements as humans. They have built incredible buildings, saved millions of lives, and even put our species on the moon! But every machine needs its parts, big and small, to work smoothly with one another. When everything is "well-oiled," look out, because the potential is endless. Thus is the same with unified teams. When all parts are working in unison, growth becomes an inevitable result. Not only does the team grow more closely together, but the individual learns more about himself or herself by working to improve for the sake of the team. The greatest teams need great individual effort, and exceptional individuals need elite teams!

Sharpen Your Edge

REGARDLESS OF HOW THE QUESTIONS BELOW ARE ANSWERED, THEY SHOW THE IMPORTANCE OF WHAT CAN AND CANNOT BE CONTROLLED. WHAT YOU CONTRIBUTE TO THE TEAM WILL IMPACT YOUR TEAM IN ONE WAY OR ANOTHER.

1. WHAT AM I WILLING TO SACRIFICE FOR MY TEAM?

2. WHAT IS MY TEAM WILLING TO SACRIFICE FOR ME?

3. WHAT DOES THAT SAY ABOUT MY TEAM?

MOMENTUM IS GENERATED BY THE BEST OF TEAMS. HOW IMPORTANT is it?

Baseball. America's pastime. The beginning of professional athletes in America started with Ty Cobb and Babe Ruth, both legends of their time and well beyond. Ty Cobb is one of the greatest hitters of all time and played in three consecutive World Series with the Detroit Tigers, losing all three. Babe Ruth was the home run king of baseball, but his New York Yankees won seven American League pennants and four World Series titles. Both players were clearly on excellent teams, so what set them apart? Momentum.

In athletics, there might not be a more fun thing to watch than a "hot" team. The Colorado Rockies made it to the World Series for the very first time in 2007. Their run to the National League pennant and the October classic might be one of the greatest team achievements of all time. By winning 14 of their last 15 regular season games and a one-game playoff to secure the NL Wild Card, the Rockies were on fire heading into the playoffs. They then swept the Philadelphia Phillies in three games. THEN, they beat the Arizona Diamondbacks in four straight games to go to the World Series. So it was only natural that they won out to become the kings of the baseball world, right? Nope. They were swept in four games by the Boston Red Sox.

Boston had to come back from a 3-games-to-1 deficit in the American League Championship series. They scored 30 runs in the last three games of that championship series, then 29 runs in four games to win it all. The problem for the Rockies? They were on fire for over a month and a half, then had to wait for the winner between Cleveland and Boston. They lost their team momentum. Boston had to find their team mojo to even make the World Series. It carried the Red Sox to a championship.

How does momentum work in the non-sports world? The same way it does in athletics: belief. Everyone, from small groups of people to large organizations, need to have a larger purpose to believe in to be effective and successful. In terms of momentum, it's all about what the people involved believe. Are most of the team members positive, hard-working, and focused on the things they can control and contribute to the group? Are they negative, lazy, and disconnected? Both groups will affect the momentum of the group. In Alan Stein Jr.'s book *Raise Your Game*, he describes how each individual affects the belief or momentum of any group:

"Skepticism and uncertainty, even inside one person, can create huge problems for a team. The reason? Because it never stays there. It will spread, sap the group's spirit, and drain their belief in what they are doing... Doubt and negativity are incredibly contagious. Fortunately, so are enthusiasm and belief."

There are few things that can stop a united team. By working in small cohesive units, teams build their confidence and create a collective mindset. The mindset that they are unbeatable spreads throughout the team, and only a bad break or an interruption of the momentum can change that. Unfortunately, the opposite can occur as well. A negative vibe or expectation within a team can spread like wildfire. Momentum can push you over the top or bury you to unescapable depths. That's why the health of the individual and the units within the team are so critical to track and observe.

WHILE IN THE FIRE, "THE TEAM" LOOKS...

DISTRACTED

Individuals pulling in different directions, momentum-killing events, and a lack of communication, can all disrupt team unity.

LOST

Individuals who don't understand the purpose and vision of the group damage the team's potential. Unity requires not only the best of every individual, but enhances those abilities to maximize the talents of each person in the group.

SELFISH

Individuals who only focus on the positive outcomes for themselves lose sight of the bigger picture. They often fall short of meeting their potential and frequently derail others from achieving their best.

WHEN "THE TEAM" IS FORGED, IT WILL...

ESTABLISH ROUTINES

Develop routines for the individuals and groups within your team, classroom, family, or organization. Planned actions, for short and long-term goals, keep everyone sharp and ready for quick adjustments. Confidence is the fuel of momentum. When momentum is achieved, routines and processes allow it to continue.

PROVIDE VISIONARY LEADERSHIP

For a group to have unity, the leaders within the group must help the others to "see" where they are heading. Individuals must know their roles and execute their responsibilities to the best of their ability. Vision, missions, and goals all clarify the purpose of your collective work. See where you are going, and the path will present itself.

BECOME THE FIST

If we were to punch a board with just one finger, we would end up with a cast and a bruised ego. Ball the fingers into a fist, and that same board would shatter upon impact. Each "finger" must do its job to form the fist. One weak link, and your hand will break. Push the individual to become better, not for their own sake, but for the collective strength of the unit. Strong, prepared individuals become a powerful force when they combine into their group. Powerful groups create unbreakable bonds and teams.

PART VII

EXCELLENCE

Excellence is an outcome. It is a strange topic for a book about self-awareness and growth, but we believe that finding excellence gives us all an opportunity to experience a personal level of satisfaction that continues to drive us. Excellence, however, is not just for any achievement, but is reserved as a descriptor for some of the best moments of our lives.

To begin, we must accept the uncomfortable truth found in **Delayed Gratification**. What that really means is our willingness to put aside what we <u>know</u> will feel good now for what we <u>hope</u> will feel good later. That's a tough sell for many of us, and especially children. Explaining the purpose of delaying gratification and the ways to combat our impulses gives us the opportunity to move closer to excellence.

The Cave, The Ordeal, and **The Elixir** outlines in more detail what we all will face on our voyage to a better self. **The Cave** is where our greatest fears lie. **The Ordeal** is the moment when we actually confront those fears and emerge victorious, albeit bruised and battered. **The Elixir** is the gift that the hero brings back to their original world, ending the journey.

The End... Is Just the Beginning embraces the cyclical nature of achievement and excellence. When we meet or exceed one of our goals, it satisfies the initial need and desire we had to accomplish something valuable. But it also creates a drive within us to look for more opportunities to prove ourselves.

22

DELAYED GRATIFICATION

"What's the difference between the successful and the unsuccessful? The successful sacrifice."

— JORDAN PETERSON

WHAT IS YOUR FAVORITE CANDY BAR?

In the 1970s, a professor at Stanford University named Dr. Walter Mischel was curious about an idea called "delayed gratification". In essence, delayed gratification is the ability to say no to something that you really want now in order to achieve a greater reward at a later time. In this particular instance, the doc wanted to know how soon it developed in children. So, he brought unsuspecting kids into a room with a marshmallow on the table. Of course, they knew exactly what was on the table! But, before he let them dig in, he gave them a choice. Dr. Mischel told them he had to step out of the room for a moment, and they could have the marshmallow as soon as he left OR they could wait until he got back ,and they could have two marshmallows. Sounds like a dirty trick, doesn't it? I love marshmallows!

What he found was most of the kids couldn't wait and dove right in, foregoing any chance at a lovely second marshmallow. However, there were a few that could hold out for a bigger reward, and those disciplined kids got two handfuls of marshmallowy goodness. The doctors studied this idea and kept track of this same group of kids for another 20 years. You'll never guess what they discovered. Kids at a young age who had a heightened sense of delayed gratification were more likely to get better grades, go to college, and eventually get better jobs. So I have to ask, would you give up your favorite candy bar, for a while, in order to get something better later on? Oh, wait... there is a catch.

HOW DO I FIND MY EXCELLENCE?

Now that I have your attention with marshmallows, let's talk about excellence. Not so much marshmallow excellence, but excellence as a core value. Excellence is defined as "the quality of being outstanding or extremely good." We often use this word to describe objects, people, actions, and organizations that are the best in their category. It is a fitting definition. In many cases, however, there is much to understand of how something, or someone, becomes excellent.

When we observe excellent people, schools, programs, and businesses, we usually only see the final product. In most cases, we don't see the years of work, the failed attempts, and the sacrifices made in order to achieve excellence. The unfortunate reality of pursuing excellence is that it is always partnered with sacrifice. In every case, excess is trimmed in order to become the best version of itself. Think about a tree. For a tree to have the most potential to live long and look its best, it must be frequently pruned. An arborist will collect their tree trimming tools and cut off the branches that are dead or are taking away from the beauty of the tree. This is only the first half of the pruning process, however. The second half of the process requires careful planning of watering, fertilization, and ensuring conditions that allow the tree to grow and replenish what was removed. It also prevents disease and decay within the tree, establishing stronger and more viable roots. Pruning affects the exterior beauty of the tree while fortifying the essence of the interior of the tree and its strength.

The same can be true for our lives. If we are to pursue what is meaningful and try to be excellent, there must be a pruning session! Trust me, it will be painful. Just like a tree with the arborist's tools, things must be cut— with the correct tools. But the next step is where it can get really difficult. Too often people accept what is good rather than great. Excellence requires you to eliminate the good and replace it with what is great in your life. It will look different for everyone, even for your closest friends. The truth is, making individual sacrifices is the equivalent of pruning a tree. There are times where we as people must let go or remove parts of ourselves to be able to expand our roots and eventually grow "taller".

If you want excellence, then a thorough evaluation of your habits and output must be tested! Take a few moments to first think about what you want to be excellent in your life.

Sharpen Your Edge

---

1. WHAT HABITS OR ACTIVITIES ARE HOLDING YOU BACK?

2. WHAT PEOPLE ARE GETTING IN THE WAY?

3. WHAT CAN YOU CHANGE TODAY THAT WILL HELP YOU PURSUE WHAT IS MOST MEANINGFUL?

HOW DO YOU KNOW IF SOMETHING IS EXCELLENT?

Things that are excellent pass a test. If you have ever watched *Gold Rush*, you have seen the incredible amount of work that goes into mining gold. They work to find the best location. Then they find the best heavy equipment operators to work the equipment. Then comes the hours and hours of work moving tons of dirt for only a few pounds of gold. At the end of each episode, you see the exact amount of gold that was mined in either a cup or in a pan. However, this is only the beginning. What they don't show us is how they turn the gold dust into purified gold through the refining process. In order to know exactly how pure the gold is, they have to melt it and take out the impurities. The same is true of ourselves. We will spend an enormous amount of time and effort trying to morph into what we want to become. Think about the hours we spend studying, working out, and practicing to be just right. Then we are suddenly thrown into the moment. The fiery moment that tests us right to the core. That moment that tells us exactly what we are... way off the mark, almost there, or *EXCELLENT*.

If you think about the greatest challenges you have faced in your life, they always reveal our true identity. They show us our greatest strengths and expose our weaknesses. This is without a doubt a huge blessing, IF you're willing to endure it. These "tests" are like the refining process. When we get put into the fire, our impurities float to the top. If we are willing, we scoop out the bad and make our gold even better. The fire is much like the pruning of ourselves; it hurts. But let's make one thing crystal clear... suffering and struggle is inevitable, but the outcome produces something beautiful and precious!

WHILE IN THE FIRE, DELAYED GRATIFICATIONS LOOKS LIKE...

A LACK OF GOALS

There is nothing worse than painfully experiencing sacrifice without a purpose. Unfortunately, this is where many of us find ourselves while enduring difficult situations. Why would anyone intentionally sacrifice something they want, just to suffer? You'd have to be a little off your rocker! On the contrary, those who have goals find it much easier to give up things they want now for something more valuable in the future.

INSTANT GRATIFICATION

The greatest threat to personal development is the inability to say no to temptations right now. Marketers, social media companies, and other business leaders have become masters of manipulation. In fact, I would bet that your social media (cell phone) has been tempting you to look at it in the last few minutes... or until you hear or feel a new notification! We live in a world of instant gratification. The more we gratify ourselves with the moment to moment decisions, the less actual control we have over our lives.

BOREDOM

Proverbs 16:9 says, "Idle hands are the devil's workshop." When we are bored, we are much more likely to indulge in things that tear us down rather than build us up. How many times have you found yourself binge watching television, not knowing six or seven hours have gone by? Whew! I'm glad I'm not the only one! Here we go again. Not having a plan to work leads us down an unproductive path. Not having a plan is a recipe for only accepting the good and not challenging yourself for greatness!

WHEN DELAYED GRATIFICATION IS FORGED, IT WILL...

FIND MEANING IN WHATEVER THEY ARE DOING

If you can find meaning in what you are doing, then delaying gratification can become easier. Knowing why you are doing something creates purpose. Purpose creates consistent behavior, and excellence requires consistency. People who constantly evaluate themselves to make themselves better and naturally work toward excellence. In doing so, they work to make those around them better.

SET GOALS

The easiest way to combat mediocrity is to set goals that stretch you as a person. Goals that are specific, attainable, and time sensitive are the best. Nothing helps motivation like a little pressure, and if it's not self-induced, you are giving your power away to someone else! Take some time to write what you would like to accomplish and what you think it might take (a.k.a sacrifice) to accomplish those goals.

FIND LIKE-MINDED PEOPLE

As a species, we need human-to-human interaction. As you grow older, you find yourself drawn to people more and more like you. If you were anything like me as a kid, you probably wondered what it would take to be like "so-and-so." Better yet, what it would take to achieve "such-and-such." I will tell you from years of experience, I don't know... but it's a lot easier to try if you don't have to do it on your own. There are plenty of people in the world who have similar aspirations, with a little different way of thinking about them. The more you associate with people of the same mind, the more likely you are to achieve your goals! AND... it's way easier to delay gratification with others who will do the same!

KNOW THEIR ABSOLUTES

I think it is easy to dream about what we would like to do or become. I bet you could even list a few things that you would need to give up for a while or start doing to get closer to that person you want to be. Have you ever thought about what you can NEVER do? I would consider these your non-negotiables. If you want to be the captain of a team or club, are you willing to, say, maintain the code of conduct? Are you willing to ensure your homework is done? Are your workouts completed in full? Having a list of unbreakable rules for your life may help you define what you are willing to sacrifice.

23

THE HERO'S CAVE, ORDEAL, AND ELIXIR

"You know, when real trouble comes, your humanity is awakened. The fundamental human experience is that of compassion"

— JOSEPH CAMPBELL

WHY ARE WE ALL AFRAID OF THE CAVE?

Most human mythology stories involve a monster in a cave. The hero of the journey must walk into that dark, foreboding abyss to confront the great unknown. In reality, the hero usually knows what they will have to face. It is more about having the courage to enter. As Luke Skywalker continues his training with Yoda, he is forced to confront Darth Vader after entering the cave. Hercules must cross the river Styx (a different cave) to save Megara from Hades. Moana must fight her way through coconuts and savage waters to defeat the lava demon Te Ka to save her island village. Each hero must face their greatest personal fear or obstacle to complete their ordeal in the "cave".

Many of us chose to not enter the cave. The risk is too great. The fear is too powerful. The outcome is too unknown. And for good reason. The cave represents the end of who we are in that moment. If, at the cave, we were to look back at our journey up to this point, we would see that we actually are ready for the challenge in the darkness. Our qualities, traits, and values led us here. We have had friends, family, and mentors remind us who we are and how great we can be. It has been a fight to get here, always losing something or someone valuable to us. So why do our heroes always enter the cave? To be reborn.

WHAT HAPPENS IN THE CAVE?

In mythological terms, the hero confronts their greatest fear in the cave. Many times, this fear is called our "inner dragon." It can take many forms, but it is always a deeply personal experience and connection to the hero. This confrontation marks a critical point in the journey. The hero must enter this innermost cave alone. While they take the experiences and mentorship they have gained into the cave with them, the confrontation is always a solo mission. By taking on this deeply personal challenge, the hero in his or her current form essentially "dies." A Greek philosopher named Heraclitus once said, "No man ever steps in the same river twice, for it's not the same river and he's not the same man." The hero who enters the cave is not the same person as the one who leaves. The gift for the hero is the truth. They now know who they are and what they must do to complete their journey. As they complete that journey, they deliver "the elixir" to those who have supported them throughout the journey.

"I'm not a hero. How can I do this?"

You're right. You're not a hero.

Yet.

Each hero to enter that cave had the perfect mix of ability and circumstance. They had the skills and desire to make a difference; they just needed the opportunity to present themselves for them to prove it. Mentors who had guided their apprentice could now step back from the problem. In doing so, the hero is forced to cross the threshold into the magical world alone and begin the journey toward their redemption while also saving their family, community, or even galaxy. The ordeals faced are the proving ground for the hero to gain the confidence needed to move forward. Hence the crucial role of the cave. It reinforces the truth that it must challenge the hero in alternative ways in order for the hero to become their "true self."

As the hero emerges from that cave (where they had to fight alone), they return to their normal world as a changed person. They possess the "elixir," or the solution to the problem that started the hero on the journey in the beginning, and the story ends with a celebration. But what we don't see is the day after. What does the hero do now? Wait for the next big adventure?

No. The hero now enters a new "cave", one that will provide the answer to the question that we all ask ourselves as well.

What does this all mean? Is it really the end for our hero? It's actually just the beginning for the new, and most important, journey that we all take. We take the path to the eventual destination of self-awareness.

UNDERSTANDING EACH COMPONENT OF THE HERO'S JOURNEY IS A massive undertaking. We have oversimplified the story to make it more accessible. A closer look at the story, can be a fun and exceedingly valuable exercise. Here are some more detailed explanations of the three topics in this chapter:

- The Cave is all about our deepest fears. The reason the cave creates so much anxiety is that deep down, people know that "the truth" lies in the cave. What is usually most interesting about that "truth" is that it EMPOWERS the hero much more than it ever endangered them. The cave discussion is excellent to demonstrate the usually false power of fear.
- The ordeal is the moment that the truth becomes that power. It is the moment when the protagonist usually has to sacrifice something or someone to continue on the journey. It also marks the moment when the hero is furthest away from where they began the journey in the "ordinary world". The ordeal is the ONLY way the main character can actually become a hero. This is a powerful and deep topic that is primed for a meaningful discussion.
- The elixir is the answer to the problem for the hero. Many times, the elixir is the hero themself, the person who "rids the land of evil" or "leads the

kingdom to prosperity". The elixir is frequently symbolic in nature. The most important part of the elixir discussion is that it is NOT intended for the hero to use for their own personal gain. Many stories take a dark twist when the hero does try to use that symbol or powerful object for themselves.

WHILE IN THE FIRE, "THE HERO" LOOKS...

HESITANT

When the moment of truth arrives, the hero must answer the call. Many times, we limit ourselves out of fear or lack of confidence, or are simply unaware of the opportunities in front of us. Hesitation lets that fleeting moment pass us by, and with it goes the path to greatness.

DESPAIRED

The cave itself is actually inside every human being. It is the most uncomfortable place we can imagine, because deep down, the cave holds the truth. We are afraid that we will find out that we aren't good enough or smart enough to complete the adventure. We stop at the entrance, not realizing "the truth" we have created for ourselves is much worse than what we encounter.

UNCERTAIN

The moment makes the man, not the other way around. Each of us will have the adventure presented to us. Instead of trusting ourselves and taking that all important first step, we let that moment pass us by.

WHEN "THE HERO" IS FORGED, IT WILL...

TRUST MENTORS

At the critical moment of decision, the champion relies not only on their ability, but what others see in them, especially their mentors. They listen to those who have been in the cave and embody the courage and faith that their mentors and friends have in them.

ACCEPT THE TRUTH

From the depths of the cave come the most challenging truths. A champion understands that this too is part of the journey. The truth cannot be changed, only accepted. Once the hero emerges from the cave, battered and bruised by that same truth, they begin down the path of redemption and return.

EMBRACE THE STRUGGLE

Anyone we would classify as a hero has shown a knack for overcoming the most overwhelming odds and circumstances. It inspires us to become our own hero, Jedi, demigod, or island queen.

24

THE END... IS JUST THE BEGINNING.

"There is only one thing I dread: Not to be worthy of my sufferings."

— FYODOR DOSTOEVSKY

ARE YOU WORTHY OF YOUR SUFFERING?

In Viktor Frankl's book, *Man's Search for Meaning*, Frankl wrestles to answer one of the most important questions in life: What is our purpose for living? He sought understanding on the topic while he and millions of other outcasts faced the horrors of mass murder, seclusion, and the emotional and physical beatings of the Holocaust. Still, Frankl was surrounded by men who found purpose in living even after everything, including their own bodies, had been taken. It was through this surreal experience that he made a few very important observations about life. First, we ALL have purpose! Yes, every single one of us. Second, suffering and struggle are inevitable parts of life. He connects to the Dostoevsky quote and expresses the importance of our attitude when faced with suffering.

Earlier in the book we discussed the importance of choosing a positive attitude, knowing it is only one of a few things we are consciously in control of all the time. The ultimate test is how our attitude is adjusted when faced with difficult circumstances. In the pursuit of excellence, we discussed sacrifice and going into the cave. It is this adversity, struggle, and suffering that challenges your attitude. So, what do you think it means to be worthy of your suffering?

The idea of suffering is a heavy topic to discuss, and it is important to identify the different types of suffering. There are two types: unintended and intended suffering. Unintended suffering is that which is out of your control. Failed relationships, death, and accidents are just a few examples of this. Intended suffering is self-imposed. Choosing to end a terrible relationship, increasing exercise time, and actively changing habits are examples we see in everyday life. If you choose to pursue anything that is meaningful, you will fail, fall short, and make mistakes, all of which bring a certain element of suffering both intended and unintended. In both cases, however, the suffering is unavoidable. Too often, people try to do everything in their power to escape the pain of suffering. We cannot structure our lives to avoid pain. In some rare instances, people try to live in a constant state of suffering. Life is not meant to inflict perpetual self-suffering. Instead, what matters is that you allow the suffering to serve a greater purpose. There must be a "why" behind your suffering. Friedrich Nietzsche wisely wrote, "He who has a why to live can bear almost any how." Understanding this "why" is what gives purpose to our sufferings. But for many, the period of suffering rarely produces a "why" at first. It is our carnal instinct to preserve and protect ourselves from pain, either emotional, spiritual, or physical. It is not until the suffering has ended that many of our "whys" prevail.

As you get older, you will experience more highs and lows in life. As with any adult, there is far more to learn during the tough times than in those of unicorns and rainbows. The more experience you gain through suffering, the easier and more quickly you can understand your "why." Those who have a "why" can endure almost any how.

It is impossible, and presumptuous, to assume that you are going to be some gallant figure bearing your suffering perfectly. Instead, you will probably be more like me: broken down, questioning yourself, hurting physically and/or emotionally, with possibly no one to talk to. Here are a couple of thoughts to think about when the time is right for you.

How are you going to allow the suffering to serve a greater purpose?

If you suffer well, it will transform you into something much greater.

"HOW DO WE KNOW WHAT NEEDS TO END FOR US TO BEGIN?"

For our struggles to have meaning, there must be a result.

What we usually cannot realize is that the end is essential for us to have a beginning. The versions of yourself that have brought you to this point of reckoning have served their purpose. Perhaps it is a childhood friendship and relationship that is outdated. Maybe it is something as simple as clothes that don't fit anymore. Whatever that "end" is, however, we must resolve it before the next stage of growth can begin. The question becomes, how do we know what parts of our lives need to go and what parts need to stay to get us through?

Looking back through previous chapters guides the way. What aspects of our life contribute to the refining of our integrity? What thoughts and habits do I have that ensure I am disciplined? Do I treat myself and others with the kindness and respect that keeps me moving forward? Have I established healthy boundaries for myself and others? Am I willing to take risks to improve upon my natural gifts?

Each of these questions and many, many more will categorize every aspect of your life. The pieces of the puzzle that don't fit will have to move to the side, if not completely off the table. Occasionally, this is something simple, like removing sugar from your diet or drinking more water to improve your mental and physical wellbeing. Other times, it is an extremely difficult decision, like when you tell a long-time friend it might be in your best interest to not be close friends anymore. While it is certainly difficult, it's an important step in the process on the way to achieving excellence.

The important thing to remember is that this process usually takes time, as it should! Eliminating outdated, damaging, or unnecessary clutter from your mental or physical world is necessary. Consider that growth period a positive indicator of your refinement, your values, and future goals. The ending of one story is just the beginning of another.

. . .

HOW DO I KNOW I'VE EARNED THIS?

You have suffered. You have faced fears, failures, disappointments, and doubt. You understand and live "the code." Respect, integrity, and pride exude from your presence. You are gracious, humble, and kind. You are disciplined, courageous, and a beacon of unity. You are the embodiment of excellence. You have reached the end! You graduate, you marry, you have children, etc. And what has it all been for?!? You! It's all for you. But then something happens.

It's not. It's not for you at all. At that very moment, you are no longer the "you" of old. A new "you" has emerged and now stands before those very people and institutions that have been with you the entire time. Parents, grandparents, siblings, teachers, coaches, pastors, and friends all show up to witness the birth of the new you. And at that moment, it all makes sense. Everything that you did was actually to prepare you to be of service to those around you. The day of your high school graduation is about you. The next day is the first day that you use that new title of "graduate" to do more. Maybe you can make more money for your family with a better job. Perhaps you can now go to college and get the degree that will let you fill a need in your society. Even your experiences in school can lead to you becoming a tutor, so you can assist others to achieve their goals.

"Surge aut sis eques in nomine Dei"or "Stand up as a knight, in the name of God". Our greatest achievements in life are not for us. They can certainly be things that make us improve and feel better about what we do. But ultimately, what we become is most important and valuable in the way we can serve others. The Latin quote above is what a king or queen would say to a person about to become a knight. They have clearly demonstrated all the qualities that a person must exhibit to earn that honor. When they are knighted, they become a new person. That new person inside the armor is now the champion of all the people in the community. A champion steps forward to defend the honor and ensure the safety of the very people that bestowed him with the honor. Knighthood isn't about the knight; it's about what he represents and the purpose he serves for those around him in the "kingdom." The knight is the example of the best we can become.

Excellence personified.

WHILE IN THE FIRE, SUFFERING LOOKS LIKE...

SELF-BLAME

Suffering is brutal. Everyone must go through the full cycle of suffering. Sometimes, you may be the cause for your own suffering. Here, you must acknowledge the mistake, come to terms with how it happened, and do your best to make sure it doesn't happen again. Walking around with a dark cloud of pity over your head does nothing but isolate you from people who can help.

LACK OF MENTORSHIP

I believe it is natural to isolate yourself when going through trials and tribulations in life. There is a part of us that must reconcile what is happening or what has happened with our current state. For some, this period lasts a long time (years) and for others, it is much shorter. In both instances, it is profoundly important to find someone to help walk you through your emotional journey. These people are key for finding purpose in our suffering. They can speak to us in ways that help us process the impossible.

TIME

It takes time to reconcile situations that are difficult in life. Sometimes it takes much longer than you might think. No matter how long it takes, it will require work. REALLY. HARD. WORK. You may spend all your time wishing the suffering would go away, wishing things would change, or wishing the suffering had never happened to you. Unfortunately, doing so will undoubtedly make the struggle last longer than it needs to.

When Suffering is Forged, it will...

Commit

Plain and simple: Commit to a cause. Whatever it may be and for whatever time it may take, your cause will give you motivation to deepen your commitment. Being committed to something of value not only speaks to your worth, but to the values you possess as a person. When you fully commit, you will naturally pull others along.

Have courage

It would be easy to say that people are consistently doing what is right and honorable ALL THE TIME. You and I both know this will never happen. It takes courage to do what is right; it takes courage to say no to the things you want; it takes courage to bite your tongue and NOT say how you really feel.

Allow the "old" them to fade away

Becoming a Knight meant parts of the old you died. If you decide to embody the values of an institution, you give up some of your old ways of living. These "sacrifices" can be very difficult, but the benefits of trust, unity, and honor will be viewed by others as invaluable. In fact, there are few things more honorable than being the living embodiment of something greater than yourself.

PART VIII

GRATITUDE

It's the end of the movie. The credits roll, you sneak one last bite of popcorn, and you leave the theater. Sometimes movies make our cheeks hurt from laughing; other times we try to quickly wipe away a tear before anyone else sees. But every so often, we see a movie that stays with us well beyond the parking lot and a cup of coffee afterward. It's not just one part of the show that moved us; it's each of the pieces, when added up, that become nearly overwhelming.

As we think back, the most poignant pieces of our lives are always attached to the emotion we felt in that moment. It doesn't matter what emotion we felt; it is *that* we felt that matters. When we finish our first journey toward understanding ourselves better, we gain knowledge of three very important things:

. . .

We know that gratitude is actually the skill of happiness.

We know that gratitude is an outcome of our efforts and sacrifices.

We know that gratitude marks the end of the journey.

Enjoy the end, because, as you now know, it is just the beginning.

25

THE GIFT OF GRATITUDE

"Gratitude is the skill of happiness."

— MARK MANSON

THE PURSUIT OF HAPPINESS HAS BEEN TALKED ABOUT MANY times since it was enshrined in American history via the Declaration of Independence. Freedom was the goal of that declaration. Freedom of choice, action, and belief. Economic freedom. Political freedom. The freedom to choose our future. With that right guaranteed, happiness was in the hands of the newly christened citizens of the United States of America.

How has that chase evolved since 1776? As our societies settled, grew, and expanded, Americans pushed the barriers of science, the social contract, and geographical borders. Each time they took the first step toward a new version of freedom, it gave adventurers a renewed opportunity to feel the rush of excitement found in chasing their dreams. As the opportunities for those expansions decreased, everyday citizens were forced to find alternative paths to explore to find their happiness. Happiness was something that had to be searched for as well— something to seek, something to practice. When those people who found their happiness actually worked at it, they were developing the ability to feel and express gratitude. Gratitude is the skill (practice/habit) of happiness.

Actively working toward happiness lets you see and feel the aspects of your life that you appreciate the most. Many times we focus our gratitude on bestowing thanks to someone for a gift or a kind gesture. It is almost always a planned event, like writing thank-you notes a few days after Christmas. It completes the cycle of give and take, making everyone involved feel good about what they did. They are happy because they are grateful. What would happen if we could take that effort and place it in our daily routine?

Gratitude becomes a skill, something that we have practiced enough to be better at than we once were. It can become one of our core values, and turning it into action leads to it being a virtue. Being thankful is a gift. And gifts are meant to be shared and given away. It costs you nothing.

GRATITUDE IS AN OUTCOME.

Gratitude grows as our lives become more intertwined with one another. We find friends who share our interests, and we are thankful to feel like we belong. We find a partner, and we are grateful for the feeling of love and being loved. Other people find colleagues at work who share a passion for excellence and learning, and we appreciate the chance to grow with them. Our lives become the great puzzle to be completed. We search out each individual piece. Sometimes they fit right away; sometimes they need to be put to the side to be used later. Every so often we lose a piece that we try to find, but sometimes it's just gone, and we know we will never be complete. But we keep going, seeking those pieces that make that picture as complete as it can be.

We can only see the complete puzzle when we step back and take a peek at how far we have come. We each can see the individual pieces, but we also need to see how they have all come together to make something beautiful: ourselves. We are the sum of our greatest pieces. At that moment of discovery, it overwhelms us to see how many pieces we collected: some faded or damaged, but they fill their place and keep us together. And this is when gratitude takes on a completely different meaning.

We realize that while we were pursuing our happiness, we collected the best from many, many different people who gave a "piece" of themselves to us—a gift, so that we may complete our own puzzle. We understand that happiness and thanks are most sincere when we acknowledge we never could have made it on our own.

Think of every speech we see at an awards ceremony. When someone reaches that pinnacle moment in their life, a moment that doesn't happen all that often, they immediately think of all the things that had to happen specifically for them to even be standing there. They remember each of those pieces that built their picture. In this moment, they gush with the most sincere thanks and appreciation that they may have ever felt. "The list is too long," they say, "...too many people to mention at once." They finally understand that this is something they never could have given themselves. It took everything to get to that place in their lives, and they now see that they aren't standing alone. They never were.

Sharpen Your Edge

HAVE YOU EVER THOUGHT ABOUT WHO YOU WOULD THANK IF YOU WERE TO ACHIEVE YOUR GOALS OR BE RECOGNIZED FOR YOUR WORK? WHAT ABOUT YOUR EULOGY? WHAT WILL PEOPLE SAY ABOUT YOU WHEN YOU ARE GONE?

THE ANSWERS TO THESE QUESTIONS CLARIFY HOW WE PERCEIVE THE VALUE OF OTHERS, THE IMPORTANCE OF OUR INNER CIRCLE OF PEOPLE, AND WHAT WE WILL BE REMEMBERED FOR. USE THE FOLLOWING PROMPTS TO DEEPEN UNDERSTANDING OF THESE CONCEPTS.

PRACTICE WRITING A SPEECH OF GRATITUDE

○ WHO WOULD YOU THANK?

○ WHAT ABOUT THAT PERSON OR GROUP MADE YOU THINK OF THEM TO THANK?

○ WHAT MESSAGE WOULD YOU END WITH? (WHAT ONE THING WOULD YOU WANT TO SAY TO THE WORLD?)

PRACTICE WRITING YOUR EULOGY

○ WHAT WILL PEOPLE REMEMBER MOST FONDLY ABOUT YOU AND YOUR PERSONALITY?

○ WHAT DID YOU CONTRIBUTE TO THE GROUPS OF PEOPLE THAT YOU SPENT THE MOST TIME WITH?

○ WHAT WILL YOUR LEGACY BE?

GRATITUDE IS THE END.

When it is all over, you will cry. You won't cry out of fear or happiness. You will cry because everyone, and everything, that came together for you to experience that moment vanishes forever. The experience will never happen in that exact way ever again. The end of a season, a beautiful concert, a well-lived life, high school graduation, a book, you name it. Whenever we receive the gift of the end, we know *it is a moment,* and we are overcome with gratitude. We don't want to leave the arena, field, stage, or hospital, because we know it is passing us by with each breath. How can we be overwhelmed with a feeling of thanks when we are crying and hugging away every ounce of our energy and emotion?

It's quite a simple answer. We are not built to handle any of these things on our own.

Gratitude grows into becoming gracious, or one who looks to share that experience with others. This feeling of grace embeds itself into every aspect of our lives. It changes our view of our world and those around us. More importantly, we must be gracious enough to recognize that we ourselves have grown and changed. We have become more aware of who we are and what we want to become. And for that, we are grateful.

NOTES

2. Honor

1. A common theme throughout each chapter is the importance of having a mentor. The truth is, there are many, many people who do not have someone that they can talk to and get advice from. One of the most important assignments we created in our leadership course was to require students to seek out a mentor, have discussions with them twice a month, and journal about the conversation. The results were remarkable, but there were still many students who struggled to find that go-to person.

   Build a network of people who can help provide wisdom and insight to living a more purposeful life. Close family, friends, teachers, coaches, aunts and uncles, are all great assets when it comes to mentorship.

   (An obvious step in this process is to ensure the safety of the student/child, so be sure each mentor involved has an excellent record of helping children. in a classroom setting, provide this information to the parent/guardian, making them aware of who the mentor is and the purpose of the activity).

8. Discipline of Control

1. Of the many discussions we had during the development of the book, one of the most impactful was the continued emergence of how important our relationships were to becoming more self-aware. As we add people into our lives, it is for a specific reason, even if we don't actually know what that reason is. And it doesn't always mean that these are positive people or influences. We eventually started calling these people "hole-fillers". Our flaws, desires, and dreams all expose "holes" in our development. In order to feel more "complete", we seek out people we think can meet those needs.

   A deeper understanding of "self" lets us realize how each of those people in our lives have contributed to our evolution as a person. Relationships always teach us about others, but they teach us more about ourselves. This is a powerful realization for people and one that can have a tremendous influence on how we perceive our own growth.

12. Boundaries and Kindness

1. Boundaries are a challenging subject to talk about. As individuals, our initial understanding of boundaries comes from our families, specifically our parents. We take those boundaries with us everywhere we go, and they are constantly being challenged by the boundaries (or lack thereof) of others. The more we become aware of our own boundaries, the more we can refine them. These interactions with others are insightful. Identify the values and boundaries that you appreciate the most from your family. Then brainstorm things you have seen from other people that you think are positive values or boundaries that they would instill in their own families. Often, you will want to focus on the boundaries you don't like and the discussion can get ugly fast. Using positive trait identification can mitigate the negativity.

20. The Unit

1. It's easy to fall into the trap of sports analogies, but don't let that stop the conversation. People are all different. Meet people where they are. People of all ages play video games with each other online. Talk to them about how teamwork is the only way they can win.

   We also have units within our social groups (church, school, club, etc). Find out what activities are offered in your communities and find out how you can join.

   Small community service projects are another excellent idea. Working at a local food bank or volunteering at a hospital or assisted living center are great ways to work in a low-pressure environment. Our best results come when we identify needs within the community and help to solve the problem. Small groups are perfect for projects of this nature.

ACKNOWLEDGMENTS

I would like to begin by thanking my parents and sisters for creating a home that embodied love, growth, and values. Family and relationships are the key to building a quality life, and I was fortunate to grow up surrounded by people who loved me enough to know I could always do better.

I would also like to thank my wife, Heather, for constantly being a source of inspiration, discussion, and a different perspective on how to help kids and adults alike. You are far more brave and courageous than I am, and I appreciate that about you more than you will ever know.

An immensely important part of developing the book was working with students and colleagues at Natrona County High School in Casper, WY. Young people will consistently amaze you if you give them the chance to work things out and feel like they have a voice that is appreciated and heard. Thank you to the thousands of students and athletes who allowed me to grow with you. I also appreciate the feedback and encouragement from staff members as we developed our character education curriculum. I hope that you all see a part of yourselves within these pages.

Finally, I would specifically like to thank Sommer Grogan, Heather Wetzel, Jared Swenson, Jason Butler, Ellie Sams, and Elle Botz for their tireless work in reading, editing, and improving our final product. As it should be, the last draft looks much different from the first, and the enhancements and organization of the book directly result from your feedback and professional skills. We simply could not have done it without you and your efforts. I am eternally grateful.

– Brent

I am so very fortunate to grow up in a home filled with love and support. I am immensely grateful for my parents, Mike and Jane, and my brother Tim, for the years of continuous encouragement and love you have given me. No matter the challenge, I have always felt your nudges to keep me going.

I am the luckiest man in the world to have my wife, Sommer, by my side. The loving support you have given to me through all my endeavors has been nothing short of amazing. You have taught me the value of communication, which I cherish with you every day. Thank you for your consistency, selflessness, and vision for our lives. Without you, I would wander aimlessly.

Becoming a man with purpose takes mentorship. I am blessed to have had so many great mentors in my life. Coaches Steve Harshman, Tyrone Fittje, Scott Schutte, Rick Zimmer, and Randy Larson molded a young man into a man with purpose. Ernie Mecca, Bob Young, Ken Fraizer, Jason Dillon solidified my walk with Christ. My colleagues Josh Propp and Brent Jurgensen have taught me how to be a great friend. Without all of you, this book would never exist. Thank you for the years of commitment to my life. You have all been a beacon of servant leadership to thousands. I was lucky to be one of them.

In the years we spent developing this book, there were a few people who willingly helped sharpen our focus with this book. Most notably, author Elle Botz, whom we owe so much, for your mentorship in becoming authors. To those who helped read, edit, and fix many of our mistakes—Thank You!
    – Tom

BIBLIOGRAPHY

Wholeness

Using a car analogy.
Manson, M. (2020). *Everything is f*cked: a book about hope.* Harper.

The Statue of Liberty.
U.S. Department of the Interior. (n.d.). *Statue Of Liberty National Monument (U.S. National Park Service).* National Parks Service. https://www.nps.gov/stli/index.htm.

"The New Colossus".
U.S. Department of the Interior. (n.d.). *The New Colossus.* National Parks Service. https://www.nps.gov/stli/learn/historyculture/colossus.htm.

Honor

Code of Chivalry.

Knights Code of Chivalry. (n.d.). http://www.lordsandladies. org/knights-code-of-chivalry.htm.

Darth Vader, Jedi, Yoda.

20th Century Fox ; Lucasfilm Limited production ; written and directed by George Lucas ; produced by Gary Kurtz. (2013). Star wars. Episode IV, A new hope. Beverly Hills, Calif. :20th Century Fox Home Entertainment

Virtues

Plato and Socrates.

Plato. (2008, August 27). *The Project Gutenberg Ebook of The Republic*. Index of /files/1497. https://www.gutenberg.org/ files/1497.

As Rumi said.

Chester, C. (2017, December 7). *A Path To Healing: The Wound is the Place Where the Light Enters You*. HuffPost. https://www. huffpost.com/entry/a-path-to-healing-the-wou_b_7916968.

Self-Esteem and Failure

CALL OF DUTY

Trademark of Activision Publishing, Inc. - Registration Number 3957781 - Serial Number 85138365 :: Justia Trademarks.

Every time we attempt new try's...

Rogan, J. (Host). (2018, November 29). Jordan Peterson (1208)

[Video Podcast Episode]. In *The Joe Rogan Experience*. https://www.youtube.com/watch?v=vIeFt88Hm8s

Questions about Failure -
Power, Rhett. "5 Keys to Great Decision-Making." *Inc.com*, Inc., 22 Feb. 2017, www.inc.com/rhett-power/5-keys-to-great-decision-making.html.

Compare and Despair -
Bolton, J. (2010, August 09). How to wreck your self esteem: Compare yourself with others. https://www.psychologytoday.com/us/blog/your-zesty-self/201008/how-wreck-your-self-esteem-compare-youself-others

Accepting Compliments -
Rane, Z. (2020, September 16). The psychological reason you hate receiving compliments. https://medium.com/psychobabbling/the-psychological-reason-you-hate-receiving-compliments-fea747c7de30

Sacrifice

John Maxwell on Sacrifice -
Maxwell, J. (2016, May 24). The power of sacrifice. https://www.johnmaxwell.com/blog/the-power-of-sacrifice/

Flex your no muscle -
Morgan, N. (2017, December 07). Are you afraid to flex your "no" muscle? https://www.huffpost.com/entry/are-you-afraid-to-flex-yo_b_8855000

Achievement

Not today, but not forever -

Family matters message by Andy Stanley [Video file]. (2017). United States: North Point Resources. https://vimeo.com/222848474

Discipline of Self

To be statements -

Balancing life's Demands: Biblical Priorities for a Busy Life [Video file]. (2011). United States: Living on the Edge. https://livingontheedge.org/group-studies/balancing-lifes-demands/

Results based on Identity not outcome -

Clear, J. (2019). *ATOMIC HABITS: An easy and proven way to build good habits and break bad ones*. New York, NY: RANDOM House BUSINESS.

Wake up, get right to work

McRaven, W. H. (2017). *Make your bed*. London: Michael Joseph.

Discipline of Control

What you can control -

Epictitus, & Lebell, S. (1994). *The art of living: The Classical manual on Virtue, Happiness, and Effectiveness*. New York, NY: HarperCollins.

Discipline of Reflection

A good habit is started by making it obvious -

Clear, J. (2019). *ATOMIC HABITS: An easy and proven way to build good habits and break bad ones.* New York, NY: RANDOM House BUSINESS.

What would happen if you placed your backpack -

Fogg, B. J. (2020). *Tiny habits: + the small changes that change everything.* Boston: Houghton Mifflin Harcourt.

Noise and distractions -

Gallo, A. (2018, April 03). What to do when you're feeling distracted at work. Retrieved from https://hbr.org/2017/12/what-to-do-when-youre-feeling-distracted-at-work

Find your space -

Shetty, J. (2020). *Think like a monk: Train your mind for peace and purpose every day.* New York: Simon & Schuster.

Manners

They are safe, easy to work with -

Packer, A. J. (2014). *How rude!: The teen guide to good manners, proper behavior, and not grossing people out.* Minneapolis, MN: Free Spirit Publishing.

Manners are not like coats -

Wiggin, E. (1884). *Lessons on Manners: For School and Home Use.* Boston: Lee and Shepard.

Look for the positive -

Cacioppo, J. T., Cacioppo, S., & Gollan, J. K. (2014). The

negativity bias: Conceptualization, quantification, and individual differences. *Behavioral and Brain Sciences, 37*(3), 309-310. doi:10.1017/s0140525x13002537

Courtesy

Courtesy is all about actions -
Patton, J. (2018, November 10). The lost art of common courtesy. Retrieved from https://iamjustinpatton.medium.com/the-lost-art-of-common-courtesy-3a5b9df98a48

Boundaries and Kindness

On a personal level, your boundaries -
Brown, B. (2010). *Gifts of imperfection, the:* Hazelden Information & Educational Services.

Without a realistic view of our boundaries -
TEDxTalks (Director). (2015, December 17). *Good boundaries free you | sarri gilman | tedxsnoislelibraries* [Video file]. https://www.youtube.com/watch?v=rtsHUeKnkC8

Generosity and Kindness

It originally meant to be of noble birth -
University of Notre Dame. (n.d.). Science of generosity. Retrieved from https://generosityresearch.nd.edu/more-about-the-initiative/what-is-generosity/

She participated in an excellent podcast -
Brand, R. (Host). (2019, June 23). In *Under the Skin.* Retrieved from (https://podcasts.apple.com/za/podcast/85-vulnerability-and-power-with-bren%C3%A9-brown/id1212064750?

i=1000442345382

Find a Passion -
O'Hagan, E. (2005). Generosity and Mechanism in Descartes's Passions. Retrieved from http://www.minerva.mic.ul.ie/vol9/descartes.html

Integrity and Kindness

This can lead us to say and do -
Simons, T. (2002, February 01). Behavioral integrity: The perceived alignment between managers' words and deeds as a research focus. Retrieved from https://ecommons.cornell.edu/handle/1813/72198

Regardless of where you begin -
Caldwell, C. (2017). Understanding Kindness – A Moral Duty of Human Resource Leaders. *The Journal of Values-Based Leadership, 10*(2). doi:0733.102.1188

Know the importance of habits
Clear, J. (2019). *ATOMIC HABITS: An easy and proven way to build good habits and break bad ones.* New York, NY: RANDOM House BUSINESS.

Respect

According to the Oxford Dictionary -
Respect. (2021). In *Oxford Online Dictionary.* Retrieved from https://www.oxfordlearnersdictionaries.com/us/definition/american_english/respect_1#:~:text=Advanced%20American%20Dictionary-,respect,greatest%20respect%20for%20your%20brothe

Creating boundaries for yourself -

Camins, S. (2021, January 22). Setting emotional boundaries in relationships. Retrieved from https://roadtogrowthcounseling.com/importance-boundaries-relationships/

Consistency -

Gray, A. E. (2020, November 25). "The Common Denominator of Success". Retrieved from https://jamesclear.com/great-speeches/the-common-denominator-of-success-by-albert-e-n-gray

Fight your Fear

No Regrets Commercial-

Sorry about Your Tattoo [Advertisement]. (2015, May 21). Retrieved March 18, 2021, from https://www.ispot.tv/ad/7hWf/milky-way-sorry-about-your-tattoo

Crossing the Threshold -

Campbell, J. (2012). *The hero with a thousand faces* (3rd ed.). New World Library.

Talents and Aptitudes

Masters have organized their days.

Gladwell, M. (2009). *Outliers*. Harmondsworth: Penguin.

Fail Your Way to Greatness

Engineering myself small.

Brown, B. (2013, July). *Listening to Shame* [Video]. TED-Ed Global. https://youtu.be/7jtZdSRst94

The One

T.H.I.N.K.

Olson, R. (2015). *Legacy builder: Five non-negotiable leadership secrets*. Cross Training Publishing.

The Unit

Current business leaders

14 Common Qualities Employers are Looking For. Indeed Career Guide. (n.d.). https://www.indeed.com/career-advice/finding-a-job/qualities-employers-want.

NFL teams.

Hobson, G. (2020, April 26). *Bengals Raft of 'A' Draft Grades Courtesy of Captain's 'C'*. The Bengals received high grades from the media and draft gurus for their 2020 draft class. https://www.bengals.com/news/bengals-raft-of-a-draft-grades-courtesy-of-captain-s-c.

As it pertains to physics.

Encyclopædia Britannica, inc. (n.d.). *Cohesion*. Encyclopædia Britannica. https://www.britannica.com/science/cohesion.

You can push only to the level of trust.

Meyer, Urban. *Above the Line*. Penguin Publishing Group, 2015.

Observation of improvement.

*This concept is everywhere in the business/corporate world as well as in education. Call it operational efficiency or continuous improvement, it all measures the same data.

Hide their fear.

"Keep your fears to yourself, but share your courage with others." Robert Louis Stevenson.

The Cave, the Ordeal, and the Elixir

The hero of the journey.

Campbell, J., Cousineau, P., & Brown, S. L. (1990). *The hero's journey: the world of Joseph Campbell : Joseph Campbell on his life and work.* San Francisco: Harper & Row.

Luke Skywalker.

20th Century Fox ; Lucasfilm Limited production ; written and directed by George Lucas ; produced by Gary Kurtz. (2013). Star wars. Episode V, The Empire Strikes Back. Beverly Hills, Calif. :20th Century Fox Home Entertainment

Hercules.

Riordan, Rick author. (2015). Percy Jackson's Greek heroes. Los Angeles :Disney*Hyperion Books

Moana.

Clements, R., Musker, J., Williams, C., & Hall, D. (2016). Moana. Walt Disney Studios Motion Pictures.

The Pit of Despair.

Brooks, D. (2016). The road to character. Random House Trade Paperback edition. New York: Random House.

The End…. Is Just the Beginning

In Viktor Frankl's book.

Frankl, V. E. i. (1984). Man's search for meaning: an introduction to logotherapy. 3rd ed. New York: Simon & Schuster.

There must be a "why".
Nietzsche, F. W., & Large, D. (1998). Twilight of the idols, or, How to philosophize with a hammer. Oxford: Oxford University Press.

The old you must die.
Manson, M. (2018, January 25). How to Let Go [web log]. https://markmanson.net/how-to-let-go.

ABOUT THE AUTHORS

 Teacher, coach and family man, Tom Grogan's passion for leadership and character development runs deep in every aspect of his life. Growing up in Wyoming, discipline and hard work formed his foundation. Whether it's in the classroom, on the football field, or in everyday mentorship, Tom lives to teach young people about character education. In 2018, Tom received the Arch Coal Outstanding Teacher award. Shortly thereafter, he founded LIFT Wyoming, a non-profit organization promoting youth leadership throughout the state.

Tom currently lives in Casper, Wyoming with his wife Sommer and their two children, Kellan and Elise. When his soul needs realignment, a fly rod and a mountain stream magically put his world in order. You can connect with Tom on twitter at @coachgrogan52.

Brent Jurgensen is a 24 year veteran in the world of education and coaching. He is a graduate of the University of Wyoming and Chadron State University, as well as being the James Madison Fellow for the state of Wyoming in 2012. Named Coach of the Year for the State of Wyoming twice, contributed to 13 state championship teams, coached 24 individual state champions, and seven state record holders in track and field. He has also created an ethics and leadership curriculum, ventured into business ownership, and works in sports broadcasting.

Brent lives in Casper, Wyoming with his wife, Heather, and his children, Royce and Piper, while the eldest, Paisley, continues her education in St. George, Utah. He lives for his family, fishing adventures, guitar, travel, reading history, baseball, and ultimately, the pursuit of live music. You can connect with Brent on twitter at @bjurgens23.